CONVERTS IN NEW SPAIN

Alicia Gojman Goldberg

Copyright 2018 Inteliprix Ediciones

Prit edition 2020

Editor: Dersu Figueroa Zárate

Contact: dersu.figueroa@inteliprix.com

Please visit for more titles: https://www.inteliprix.com/nuestros-titulos

CONTENTS

PROLOGUE

This book originally published in the 1980s is part of the pioneering studies of the Jewish population in Mexico. The author, Alicia Gojman not only has a long and outstanding career as a historian; she has also played a significant role in the culture of contemporary Mexican Jews. She has been the promoter of a cultural project that has managed to combine important documentary collections maintained in a vital center dedicated to the study and dissemination of the Judeo-Mexican culture. She has promoted far-reaching editorial projects, in which the memories, images, documents and contributions of generations of Jews in Mexico have been combined.

In this work the author's purpose was to help remedy the absence of the Jewish people in the historiographies about Spain and the New Spain; an unjustified absence since this population was present from the origin of the Spanish kingdom. In the first part of the book, the history of the Jews in the Iberian Peninsula is shown through a long list of prominent figures that contributed to science, economics and politics. For fifteen centuries they participated intensely in this society, at their side even in war. It is clear that the Jews' contribution to the formation of the Spanish identity cannot be minimized.

During this long time there were periods of peaceful coexistence, alternating with different degrees of persecution. The fear of the attacks against them became integrated as part of the life of the Jewish population, as well as their determination to continue their culture. The author explains the importance of mysticism as the element that gave meaning to the suffering caused by the persecutions. In the end there was a divine reward.

At this stage, the cultural elements developed as well - based on religion – which would provide the Jewish population with the rules and ways of life that allowed them to adapt to the different nations in which they resided. It not only made the preservation of their own culture possible, but also the creation of a new cultural entity as Spanish Jews, as Sepharadites. An identity they carried with them when they had to leave due to the expulsion decrees.

As the Spanish State consolidated, Spanish Jews faced the dilemma of accepting conversion to Catholicism – the state religion - or losing everything or almost everything and leaving. The converts, contemptuously called marranos, had to relinquish their sacred books, stopped observing their holidays, their prayers and chants; Under these conditions, their religious practice deteriorated and in some cases it ended up disappearing.

America's discovery was taken advantage of by groups of converts, actually, Crypto-Jews, who saw in emigration to the new lands the possibility both of escaping persecution and of having greater freedom to continue practicing their religion. They were Catholics on the outside, but within the group they continued their ancient religious practices such as circumcision, fasting, observance of the Sabbath and feasts, funeral rites and dietary rules.

The author makes it clear that it was not an individual emigration and, although it is not quantified, it is clear that hundreds of families arrived in the new world and they settled in practically all of New Spain. They stood out in highly appreciated professions such as doctors, miners and merchants, among other activities. Some reached the best economic positions and had political influence, however, it was not enough to save themselves from the terrible Inquisition, as hundreds of proceedings preserved in Mexico's General Archive of the Nation show.

The author made an interesting selection of representative cases of the inquisitorial trials suffered by crypto-Jews in New Spain. Delations, trials, torments, confessions and sentences illustrate the complexity of a developing society where the religious question mixed with economic and political interests. Among the Jews who suffered dispossession and torment were young and old, men and women, of different socio-economic positions. A documentary appendix complements this pioneering work.

Studies such as this of Alicia Gojman show that the settlement of Sephardic families in New Spain was larger than commonly believed, as well as that they not only settled in Mexico City, but also reached different regions both in the north and the south of the country. Therefore, it should not be assumed that all vestiges of this crypto-Jewish culture disappeared, even more so when we have news nowadays about communities of indigenous origin such as Venta Prieta in the state of Hidalgo, which have demanded the recognition of their belonging to Mexican Jews community.

It is possible to think of moving from the isolated anecdote to the search for Sefaradite contributions in the formation of Mexican culture, together with the substratum of original American cultures, the European elements brought by the Spaniards and the contributions of the African cultures.

Guadalupe Zárate Miguel
July 2018

INTRODUCTION

When going over the historiography of Spanish history and later on that of New Spain, we find similarities between both. Jews and converts appear only in rare occurrences, having formed an integral part of the population of each of those nations. The point is that historians have no idea how to behave towards them; they know not how to focus and locate those groups in the general historical plan.

The history of Jews beginning from the fall of the Second Temple, and what is more, their exile from Israel, was not a national history. Thus, some historians state that it is not necessary to dwell on a group that is closed from within, apparently located beyond historic development. However, Américo Castro said that "Primary evidence that people have a historic dimension appears in the fact that its work is present in the life of other nations. And that is what happens in Spanish history, the constant participation of the Jewish people is evident, it is present in the development of a nation, in its historic advent, in preparing its culture."[1]

The purpose of this book is to make a short study about converts or Crypto-Jews who went to America after the Spanish discovery of this New World.

Jews and converts left indelible prints in the creation of the "Spanish being". During fifteen centuries they participated in the life and development of a nation and, later, although as converts, they continued influencing the Hispanic spirit, both in the Iberian Peninsula as well as in America. The consequences of the edict adopted by the Catholic Kings, of expelling a mass

---

[1] Castro, Américo, *La Realidad Histórica de España,* México, Editorial Porrúa, 1954, Biblioteca Porrúa, No. 4, p. 12

of cultivated, hard-working and enterprising Spaniards, were very soon reflected in the country's impoverishment.

When the Jews left Spain, an arm of commerce was eliminated just at the time when the discovery of the New World claimed the concurrence of all its energies.

Converts rooted in that culture remained for a number of reasons in Spain (mostly because they were already Christians) and they participated in the discoveries and conquests of the new territories as well as in forming part of colonial society. However, identification with their own group persisted in many cases and maturity made it easier for Jews to face many conflicting situations.

Hispanic believers lived with confidence and hope and so they altered their ideas about themselves and the vital space in which they projected their personal activities, because "being Spanish meant mainly having lived as believers."[2] Their adjustment to the environment and the circumstances, their contribution to economic, political, social, cultural and religious life of the viceroyalty is important and also forms part of the future "American being".

---

[2] *Ibidem.*

✠ Tractatus contra hereticam prauitate[m]
Et etia[m] tractatus de Irrigularitate editi:
per Gundissaluum de villa diego sacri pa
latij apostolici auditore[m]. Nouiter impressi
Ac alme correcti.   Cum repertorio.

CHAPTER I

The Spanish Jew

The Jewish people developed a series of universally accepted values in the midst of other cultures, which they were able to amalgamate to their own and enrich their knowledge.

In contact with the Spanish culture, people responded with a double process: cultural and human. They produced a culture that deeply reflected the surrounding reality as well as a certain psychological being as a result of this environment.

The Jew remained faithful to his tradition, to the cultural prototype he created in response to his environment and, very keenly, to the countries where he developed.

Faithfulness to "Sepharadism"[3] is just a specific variable of Jewish fidelity towards himself, that is, "not to forget any fatherland or country"; thus Jews are "basically someone who lives in history, much earlier than one who lives in geography."[4]

Spanish Jews honored their adopted country by having men who excelled in every branch of human knowledge. Even after the expulsion, converts, most of them Jewish inwards, continued greatly influencing the wealth of

---

[3] Sepharadism stems from the Hebrew word *Sepharad* that means Spain. This includes all those who being Jewish formed part of Spanish culture.

[4] Pérez León, "El Porqué de la Fidelidad de los Judíos Sefarditas a su Sefardismo" in *Actas del Primer simposio de Estudios Sefardíes,* first of the actions celebrated on the 25th anniversary of the Foundation of the Consejo Superior de Investigaciones Científicas, Instituto Arias Montano, Madrid, 1970, p. 147.

Spanish wisdom. Many of them went to America in spite of all the Edicts and Decrees that forbade their entry because they did not have "blood purity".[5]

When the Edict of Expulsion was issued by the Catholic Monarchs, the converts realized there was no hope of it being revoked so they began to search for a new home where they could live with more religious liberty and await there for the Messiah.

So they went towards the newly conquered lands, where they hoped to live with more tolerance, far away from the Inquisition. They were sure that the Messiah would arrive in the New World, because God had promised them that they would be redeemed together with the whole world after a great catastrophe. Calamity had arrived in the form of expulsion from their beloved Spain, which meant that human redemption was very close.

In 1492, year of the expulsion of the Jews from Spain, the history of Spanish Jewry ends and the history of converts in the New World begins.

The story of the converts in the New World begins with the discovery of America, because they participated in its exploration and colonization to a far greater degree than modern historians give credit today.

How and when Jews arrived in Spain

It is impossible to ascertain the time of arrival of the Jews in Spain. However, there is a great body of knowledge that confirms their having dwelled in the peninsula since the beginning of the Christian era. According to some research performed,[6] there were Jews in Spain since the 1st century of the Common Era.

---

[5] Catholics who had "blood purity" were those who could show that their ancestors on both sides had been Christians for three generations.
[6] Beinart, Haim, *Los Comienzos del Judaísmo Español,* Buenos Aires, Biblioteca Popular Judía, No. 62, p.1. Professor of the H.U.J leads the Project entitled "Judaic Spain".

As the moment of expulsion drew near, Jews looked everywhere for ways to remain in the country; so they began to search even then for serious investigations to prove their long-time abode in Spain and thus, their right to live in the Peninsula.

Don Isaac Abrabanel has numerous interesting comments about the arrival of Jews in Spain; his notes in the *Libro de los Reyes* have important contributions towards solving the situation. At the end of the book he states: "…Pirro brought to Spain inhabitants of Jerusalem belonging to the tribes of Judah, Benjamin, Simon, Levy and the priests, a great number of people came with him voluntarily. He led them through the sea in vessels to the Kingdom of Spain establishing them in two provinces. One is the province today called Andalusia, in a city that in those days was a great Jewish metropolis and that Jews named Lucena, name it still carries today."[7]

Abrabanel, by stressing the place names that were somehow related to biblical sites, tried to show the antiquity of Jewish population in Spain and, thus, its right to live there, the same right of the Christian Spaniards.

This argument, using the Bible, became very common as the time approached for the expulsion, since it was the best instrument that nobody could refute or doubt its veracity.

If the date of Jewish arrival in Spain cannot be pinpointed exactly, their preference for settling in the East Coast of the Mediterranean, which prevailed up to the time of the expulsion, is obvious. It can be explained because of their constant fear of persecutions which made it easier to flee in case of need and their continuous relations, both cultural and economic, with Jews elsewhere in Europe.

To confirm the antiquity of Jews in Spanish soil, there are inscriptions in tombstones that date from the first centuries of the Common Era. The oldest is a trilingual inscription on a marble structure discovered in Tarragona. The inscription indicates in first place that the Hebrew language had not

---

[7] *Ibidem*, p. 9

disappeared or been relegated, and that it was still used just as Greek, and Latin which was beginning to be used.

The Jews who arrived in Spain carried with them a heritage and a tradition that they kept throughout their sojourn. They created a new life based on their historic past but formed part of that civilization while simultaneously being different. Jewish charismatic power had gone from God to the Law of Moses and from it to the Old Testament.

The laws of the country where they lived had to be obeyed, as long as they did not ban practice of their religion. If a law demanded for the Jew to eat some religiously forbidden food, he had the right to refuse, because by so doing he was not endangering the State in any way.

The Jew in Spain created a series of laws and ways of life that allowed him to continue being Jewish despite all ups and downs and to adapt to his new homeland. These laws formulated during the decisive centuries that preceded the collapse of the Roman Empire had important effects over Jews, allowing them to identify with the Spanish people without losing their identity. They were thus able to learn how to separate Church and State.

The Talmud as the instrument of Jewish survival exercised a decisive influence that would guide them for fifteen centuries. The Jew adapted to any circumstance in every country. Instead of accepting that the five books of Moses did not have solutions for daily life, they insisted that the Bible not only included all the answers but that it had foreseen all possible issues.

Judaism became the property of lay people and anybody who studied the Bible could become its mouthpiece.

From early age, Jews learned that God should be adored with love and not from fear.

By studying the Talmud, Spanish Jews became not only jurists, but also physicians, mathematicians, grammarians, philosophers, poets and merchants.

The most terrible sins were those against God since they alienated man from his faith. They could only be expiated by authentic penitence that in Hebrew is expressed through the words "regression or reconciliation" that mean returning to God.

These are the characteristics that define Hispanic Jews and that would continue defining them by certain differences as far as religion and belief are concerned. But this would not alienate them or make adjustment more difficult. Jews adapted towards Spanish soil from the very first years of their arrival in the Peninsula.

The history of Israel was interrupted by Rome and later by the triumph of Christianity; exile and dispersion made of the Jews an appendix in the history of the nations where fate had sent them. However, Jews were always able to adapt to the point of feeling part of those countries, to love and give their life for their adopted lands just as any other citizen would.

Towards the importance, perseverance, and simulation

The history and culture of Spanish Jews, both before and after 1492, runs together with Spanish culture "to the point that if Jews were to be removed from it, its real aspect would be unimaginable. On the other hand, it is also a fact that Hispanic Jews cannot be understood if observed only as Jews and not as Spaniards."[8]

The first documented news about relations between Jews and Christians in the Peninsula date to the 4th century, before Christianity was declared the official religion of the Roman Empire. At the time, laws were enacted against relations between those two peoples.

---

[8] Pérez Castro, Federico, *Los Judíos Españoles,* Barcelona, Sayma. 1961, p. 12

The victory of Arian Visigoths in Spain in the 5th century for a short time delayed the march of combative Catholicism. Then the Goths arrived and consolidated their position in the peninsula for a long time. The population was composed of a variety of people: Romans, Goths, Roman Catholics and heretic Arian Visigoths. Jews could be found in the midst of all these people.

At the beginning, Visigoth relations with Jews were friendly, since they considered Jews as allies in their struggles against the Catholic clergy.

The civil situation of Jews in Spain was regulated by the Code of the Visigoth King Alaric II (484-507). According to this Code, Jews were legally considered an integral part of the Roman population. But there were some restrictions among which were the right to own slaves or to build new synagogues without authorization.

The situation changed in the time of Reccared I (586-601) who abandoned the Arian cult and promised to consolidate Catholicism as the only religion of the country. "Persecution against Jews began in Spain by the conversion of Reccared at the third Council of Toledo in 589 when he ordered children of mixed Christian-Jewish marriages to be baptized without their parents' consent."[9]

Reccared decided to create a unified Spain and excommunication was decreed against any religion considered heretic.

By accepting Christianity, Visigoths managed to unite Church and State. This will later explain many of the attitudes of the Spanish people, among which we find their monarchic feelings and the united actions of State and Church.

Religious unity as an ideal among Spaniards since the time of Reccared occurred gradually. The Goths merged with the Roman population. Only insignificant traces remained of pagan cults but Jews kept their beliefs.

Saint Isidore of Seville was present at the Third Council of Toledo.

---

[9] Álvarez, Jesús, *Judíos y Cristianos ante la Historia,* España, Editorial Aguilar, 1972, Col. Literaria Tolle, Lege, p. 226.

Public discussions between Jews and Christians were frequent at the time of Saint Isidore. In 613, King Sisebut decreed that Jews reluctant to adopt Christianity should leave Spain.

The Edict of Expulsion managed to exile only a small part of the Jews, because many of them converted to Christianity outwardly with the intention of keeping their religious rites in secret and returning to them when persecutions ceased. Ever since then, there have been converts with the "art of simulation"; Jews would be Catholics outdoors and Jews indoors without the appellate with which they would be known later in history.

Saint Isidore (bishop) mentions King Sisebut, stating categorically that by dictating the Edict that forced Jews to abjure the faith of their ancestors, compelling them onto a hard exile, he did not proceed scientifically, because he had used force and royal power when he should have requested by reasons of faith to attract them to Christianity.

Saint Isidore tried to show, based on logical arguments, that the prophecies about Christ's birth, passion and resurrection had already been fulfilled and all the people had been joined together under the Christian Church. He tried to stress the errors of Judaism, stating that the new people of God had received the name of Christians. Nothing separated Jews and Christians more than religion: not language, work or professions.

In spite of Bishop Saint Isidore's opposition to forced conversions, Jews were converted and continued being oppressed, closed within themselves perceiving their future only in the development of their own culture and thought.

The Councils dealt with the problem of converts, particularly those who had returned to their previous religion, compelling them to practice Christianity, authorizing confiscation of their assets and removing their children so they could be educated as Catholics. Dealings between Jews and baptized persons were forbidden, and two categories of Jews were fixed:

1. Full-fledged Jews who had never converted and who were under common restrictions of rights that should separate them from Christian society.

2. Jews, who fearful of violence had apparently converted, should be persecuted not as Jews but rather as Christians who were deviating from the correct path and who adopted Jewish heresy, that is, were Judaizers.

Thus, the synod subjected them to the Church, made them slaves of Catholic clergy and indirectly its tributaries.

From the time of King Recevint the punishment for violating Christianity had been fixed as flagellation or the stake (656). Laws were applied both to Jews and to baptized or converts, with an official ban on the practice of Judaism.

Jews lived integrated to Spanish society in form, they exercised the same professions as their neighbors, they owned fields, vineyards and olive groves; in the cities they were artisans and merchants, their vessels sailed to all Mediterranean ports since the time of the Romans. But what divided them from the surrounding population was the religious question.

In 693, Spanish ports were closed off to Jews, so they were unable to trade in Spain. Besides which, free trade was banned to them so emigration to Africa increased.

Stemming from this situation, Jews were declared slaves of the kingdom; the king had the right to distribute them as property among various owners who had to oversee that they did not celebrate Jewish ceremonies. Children were removed at the age of seven and given over to Christians for their upbringing.

Jews who were proud but whose spirit was tortured remained upright and clung to any opportunity that could mitigate this ruthless persecution.

At the middle of the century, the Visigoth kingdom was ripe for destruction. The court teemed with incessant conspiracies. The last Visigoth king ascended to his throne when Tarik the Moslem was already on the tip of Africa, facing the great rock that carries his name. The Arabic armies were moving towards the peninsula and the Jews, whether masquerading as Christians or not, awaited the conquerors as their liberators.

In 711, led by their military chief Tarik, the Berbers crossed the strait between Africa and Spain.

Christian Spain was practically submerged under the Moslem wave. The Visigoth nation disappeared as such when it seemed to be on the verge of establishing a political, linguistic, and religious union throughout the peninsula. At that point, the northern belt from Galicia to the Mediterranean split into fragments that during centuries would remain divided, each with its own peculiar language.

Moslems arrived with two strengths: political unity and the impetus of the new-born religion.

Visigoth Spain succumbed. But very soon Christian resistance started, and the Moors were forced to a border war that only ended in the 15th century.

The reconquest became a religious crusade against Islam in a process of capital importance in the history of Spain, because it kept the essential unity between the various groups in which resistance was concentrated.

Since that time, Christianity began forging the spirit of religious intolerance that would accumulate during the eight centuries of Moslem presence in Spain and that would eventually blossom once more in the 16th century.

This deep desire of evangelization, based on the early days of the reconquest, would culminate in the 16th, 17th and 18th centuries, culmination that America would help evince. Thus, the figure of a saintly man emerges in Spain as a typical character of the Spanish Middle Ages who was considered an intermediary between man and the divinity. This figure will be present continuously in the 16th century after the discovery of America.

Islamic influence made Christians adopt the idea of the Holy War as the door to eternal glory in paradise. The Saracen invaders united by a religious link belonged to various races, but in general, it was the Arabic people the ones who shaped this conglomeration.

The Jewish communities backed the invaders believing that they would be "their saviors". Both Christians and Jews, as infidels, had to pay a special tax but they were at liberty to practice any religion.

An era of liberty and opportunity opened up then in the history of Spanish Jewry. In a short time, Jews used Arabic as their vernacular language and Moslems found a convenient link between them and the Christians, granting Jews administration of the centers they occupied.

While the great Oriental center was declining, Spain was becoming the "Babylon of the West" and for five centuries it remained the leader of Jewry.

Jewish history in Moslem Spain can be divided into three stages: the first one embraces from 711 to 1002 and includes the glorious days of the Cordoba Caliphate; the second comprises the years of disorder of the Caliphate in the Tarifa kingdoms and the third is marked by the invading Almoravids and Almohads, times of persecution, intolerance and fanaticism that climaxed with the defeat of Granada by the Catholic monarchs. We can consider the first stage as collaboration and conviviality; the second as free coexistence and the third as dispersion and emigration.

The first half century of Moslem domination totally altered the political, ethnological and cultural aspect of the peninsula.

While forming their empire, the Moslems inherited a great problem: a great number of non-assimilated elements, Christians and Jews. The Christians had not understood why the Jews had not converted to their faith, now they themselves refused with the same Jewish stubbornness to convert to Islam.

When Arabic rancor against Christians and Jews for refusing to accept the new religion began to die down, the Moslems relegated the former to the category of second-class citizens and recognized the Jews as a political entity.

A period of relative peace began for the Jews. Relations with Moors and Christians were regulated. The Jews lived together in small communities called Aljamas that were not closed areas also known as Calls. "The Mosaic religion was respected in all of them and priests, mayors and judges were named by the Council (*Aljama*), constituting one in each locality, a type of Republic where everybody conspired through science and work for the benefit of the community without their being able to transfer any estate without the consent of each of the inhabitants".[10]

This curious organization had a synagogue as well as a Talmudic school. The main rabbi or supreme priest held the highest local authority. The king or caliph named the main rabbi to one or more regions or bishoprics. The institution of the Gaonim, supreme magistrates that derived from the Pumbedita and Sura Academies were superior to the main rabbi. They took care of the integrity of civil, criminal and religious laws.

When the Umayyad kingdom was established with Cordoba, Andalusia as its capital, Jews began an era of relative economic prosperity under this dynasty in which they worked in medicine, agriculture, commerce and artisanship. Jewish and Arabic wisdom and culture flourished together and influenced one another.

The real renaissance of Jewish culture began in the 10th century under the rule of Abdurrahman III (912-961) who took over the Cordoba Caliphate.

The Caliph demonstrated his utter tolerance towards people of different beliefs when, in spite of Moslem prejudice, he named a Jew as councilor and assistant in official affairs of great political importance. It seems that Hasdai Ibn Shaprut belonged to a family of good economic position that lived in the city of Cordoba.

---

[10] Amador de los Ríos, José, *Historia Social, Política y Religiosa de los Judíos de España y Portugal.* Madrid, Imprenta de T. Fortanet, 1875, p. 142.

Shaprut had been well educated in lay matters; besides Hebrew, Arabic and Spanish Romanic languages, he was well versed in Latin. The Caliph designed him head of official finances, as well as being his main mediator in diplomatic relations.

Ibn Shaprut was able to raise the Caliph's prestige in various occasions: he concluded the negotiations with the Christian kingdoms of Leon and Navarre taking advantage of their internal conflicts. He also helped develop science and literature among his fellow Jews and set the foundations for the spiritual blossoming that would soon locate Spanish Judaism at the forefront of all Jewish communities of Western Europe. Besides performing his obligations with talent, Hasdai was a man very much interested in his origins and his religion.

Since the time of the Visigoths there was a belief among Jews that in the remote Eastern regions there was a Jewish empire governed by a prince of the tribe of Judah about which Saint Isidore had written in his book *Nativitate Domini.*

Hasdai, dominated by his Judaic feelings, contacted the ambassadors of Constantine VII and one of the things he asked them was about this far away country, the land of the Khazars, if they really had a king who held true to Mosaic laws and whose entire people followed the same laws.

The messengers confirmed to Hasdai the existence of that reign, adding the information of the name of King Joseph Aben Ahron. Hasdai firmly believed that this king and his people belonged to one of the ten lost tribes (thus confirming the Talmud's and other writer's statements). With this certainty, he decided to use his authority in the Moslem court for his people and taking advantage of a delegation going from Cordoba to Byzantium, he sent an emissary to the Khazars that read as follows: "I wish to know the truth, whether there is a place in the world where the harassed people of Israel really have their own kingdom subject to nobody. If I knew it to be true, I would leave my family and would go through hills and valleys, by land and by sea to arrive at the place where my Lord, the King rules. I would observe his greatness and glory and his entourage, I would see how the rest of Israel lives in peace. I have another request: please let me know if you have any news of the end of time (when the Messiah will arrive), for whom we await while we wander from one land to another. Desolated and humbled in dispersion we have nothing to respond to those who say: every people have a country, but you have on this Earth no trace of a State."[11]

Ibn Hasdai's behavior was very important in the history of the Jewish community of Al Andalus. He was the first person to understand Judaism in its bitter exile and by having been a leader in his time.

Hasdai is the example of the multifaceted Jew, statesman, community and intellectual forerunner who later was characteristic of the Jewish communities in Moslem Spain.

In the 11th century, the Almoravid armies were on the warpath in Andalusia. Arabic Spain was divided into the kingdoms of Taifas, each one having its own Emir. The Almoravids were a type of special militia or religious institute similar to some orders consecrated to a Holy War.

When the Caliphate dissolved, Jews sought the protection of Christian monarchs who granted it gladly because their financial aid in their war policy against the Moslems was very useful.

Ever since the reconquest had begun, Moslems and Jews of the regions being occupied by the Christians had their lands and assets confiscated. Those that escaped slavery or death had to live in the "cracks of society, having no resource but to find haven in the economy, where they developed as merchants, usurers and manufacturers."[12]

After the Almohad persecution in 1148, Jewish life in Spain concentrated in the Christian areas of the peninsula.

---

[11] Dubnow, Simón, *Historia Universal del Pueblo Judío,* Buenos Aires, Editorial S. Sigal, 1951, Vol. IV, pp. 152-153; Amador, *op .cit, Vol. II, p. 427.*
[12] Puigross, Rodolfo, *La España que Conquistó el Nuevo Mundo,* Buenos Aires, Ediciones Siglo Veinte, 1965, p. 15. About usury there are various opinions. Professor Beinart explains that it was not a generalized profession.

Essentially, commerce and technology were in the hands of Moors and Jews.

Christian Spaniards, although not having participated in the Crusades, kept the crusader spirit alive within their own territory. It remained an obsession that lasted 700 years, to eliminate the infidel, idea that would cross towards the newly conquered lands.

A man who for the Jews would be like a second Shaprut appeared in the city of Granada at the end of the first half of the 11th century: Rabbi Samuel Hanagid (993-1055).

Rabbi Samuel, just as his ancestor Ibn Shaprut, served the interests of the Jewish community. He was head of the Jews in Granada and all the Spanish communities recognized his authority. He taught the Talmud and solved legal questions. He corresponded with Babylon and published several Biblical and Talmudic manuscripts for the people.

Rabbi Samuel was considered one of the founders of the renaissance of Hebrew literature in Spain.

Spanish Jewry was rising towards a bright summit. Numerous statesmen, intellectuals, scientists, philosophers, poets, mystics and moralists appeared at that time. It was a community of men and women who had been greatly influenced by Arabic culture in Spain that had merged perfectly with their own millenary tradition. They mixed freely with their Moslem neighbors and the devotion to their faith and pride in the great past of their people was not weakened by this relationship. Their basic culture was still Jewish, based on the Bible and the Talmud.

Lucena continued being an important center of Judaic studies. During the time of Samuel Hanagid, another Jew, Yekutiel, who was murdered because of political rivalry, became vizier in Saragossa.

Another important community was Denia, a port in the Western shores of Spain and residence of the Talmudist Rabbi Isaac B. Reuven Al-Bargeloni. By the 11th century, Toledo which had a population of some 4,000 Jews was conquered by the Christians in 1085 and turned into the capital of the country.

The Jew Joseph Hanasi Ferrizuel, called Cidellus or the small Cid, who was a physician and great financier was prominent in the court of Alfonso VI and he took care of his fellow Jews as well.

King Alfonso began a tradition that remained until Spanish Jewry was extinguished: court Jews, who faithful to their religion nevertheless exercised considerable authority over the inhabitants of the kingdom. In the court of Alfonso VI of Castile there were several Jews such as the physician Amram Ibn Shabid (or Shalit) who was in the service of the king as tax preceptor of Moslem vassals as well as complying with various diplomatic missions.

Despite religious prejudice, citizenship of Jews could not be denied to people who played such an important role in Spanish political life. They lived more among the Christian kings than among Moslem Taifas, but the internal form of the Aljamas had changed relatively little.

The Aljamas were independent as political entities: they paid taxes directly to the royal treasury; they had total administrative and legal autonomy under the general supervision of a royal officer.

The 12th century marks the apex in the existence of Spanish Jewry; it is the century of the great poet and philosopher Yehuda Halevy, Moshe Ibn Ezra, Abraham Ibn Ezra, Abraham Ibn Daud, Benjamin of Tudela and many other men of letters.

The life of Yehuda Halevy is a compendium of Spanish Jewry as a whole. He had great familiarity with Aristotelian theories and was well versed in neo-Platonic concepts. While attacking all philosophers inconsistent with Jewish religion he used philosophic language and made concessions to philosophers. Yehuda Halevy considered that just as there was one truth in mathematics and logics, this truth lay also within Jewish religion.

Halevy absorbed all that Lucena could give him like Hebrew, Talmud, secular subjects such as Arabic, philosophy, science, etc. and he went back to his native Toledo where he practiced medicine. His lifetime passion was always dedicated to Zion, the home of the old glory of his people.

The man whose life constitutes the clearest reflection of the cosmopolitan environment of the Jewish community, who is considered the maximum Jewish thinker and who lived in the 12th century, was Moses Maimonides or Ben Maimon. He is also known as Rambam (Rabbi Moses Ben Maimon). His influence on later generations is incalculable and is still present. He was born in Cordoba and he and his family were forced to immigrate to the city of Fez, ruled at the time by the Almohads. They remained there for a short time and continued on to Palestine but establishing themselves there was difficult so they returned to the city of Fustat, close to Cairo in Egypt.

Moses devoted himself to medicine, becoming so famous that he was named court physician to Saladin then ruling Egypt. There are legends referring to Richard the Lion Hearted trying to convince Maimonides to abandon Saladin to become his own physician instead.

He occupied the position of *Nagid,* maximum Jewish authority within the community. He used his influence to improve the lot of his people in Egypt and other cities; they were once again allowed to live in Jerusalem from where the Christians had expelled them.

There are many works of this great sage and philosopher but the best known one is his *Guide of the Perplexed,* written for those minds that were seduced by the science and philosophy of the time and found their faith incompatible with reason.

He conciliated the teachings of the Bible and philosophy in many and very diverse ways, interpreting passages in a figurative rather than literal way. He was perfectly conscious of the limits of human intellect so he did not invoke reason in every affair. He considered the study of theology and the knowledge of God, as ordered by the Bible itself, as the most important subjects. He also believed that it is necessary to study physics and metaphysics to achieve total understanding of the Almighty.

Maimonides believed it was important to explain the differences between the Moslem, Christian and Jewish religions, because Jews lived among them. So, he prepared his thirteen dogmas or articles of faith where each one was a fundamental principle of one of the three monotheistic religions or some principle by means of which Judaism differs from the other two. These thirteen dogmas very soon became and still remain as the popular definition of Orthodox Judaism. Thanks to the books he wrote as a guide for future generations and by trying to fill the vacuum of Jews keen both to learn common knowledge as well as to understand the intellectual wisdom of the time, Maimonides was known as the most enlightened man of the Golden Age of medieval Jewish history.

By 1265, only Granada and some port cities close to Cadiz remained in Moslem hands. Jews continued living a productive and relatively peaceful life in the Christian kingdoms. The monarchs of the four Christian reigns, Castile, as the largest and located at the center, Portugal to the West, Aragon on the East and tiny Navarre inserted between Castile and Aragon, did not seem very rigorous about complying with the Edicts of the Ecclesiastic Councils.

Since the middle of the 13th century, the horizon of the Spanish Jew was Castile. Jews began to write not only in Arabic, but by using Castilian, created new works.

In the court of Alfonso X there were many Jewish men of letters. The famous Alfonsine code of law was written by Ishaq Ben Cid and Yehuda Ben Moshe.

In those days, Jews were not forced to convert to Christianity, and it was forbidden to insult converts because of their origin. On the other hand, if a Christian converted to Judaism, he could be sentenced to death and his assets confiscated. Jews and Christians could not reside in the same house and Jews could not have Christian slaves. But many Christians hired Jewish teachers to educate their children.

The Aljamas turned inwards into themselves reinforcing their autonomy. Under the leadership of the muqaddamin or adelantados they established their own courts of law but retaining the right of appearing before the royal courts.

The king would name the court Rabbi, in charge of supervising community activities. Generally, this Rabbi did not interfere in the least in the internal affairs of community organizations.

Jews reached very high positions in the royal court and so the fall of any of these functionaries usually brought brutal consequences to their communities. But in the land of the Christians the habit of employing Jews in high administrative and financial positions continued.

In this environment, Jews wanted to live like nobles and competed for royal favors so great court dynasties emerged, families of great nobility within the community itself.

Salomon Ibn Zadok of Toledo known as Culema was ambassador and main customs officer. His son and successor, Isaac Ibn Zadok known as Cag de la Maleha, performed a very important role reestablishing the finances of Alfonso X.

The financial success of these administrators induced the kings to impose higher taxes on Jewish communities that became impoverished in their effort to comply with them.

The Church, the courts and the noblemen constantly disagreed with the kings because the Jews exercised undue influence in the kingdoms; the former felt that royal favor tended to benefit Jews who were rivals and competitors whose powerful arms seemed to have a hand in restructuring the monarchy.

Kings took Jews as their property and protected them so they would not be harmed unless they committed a crime. This situation was used by Christians who in retaliation would blame Jews for crimes they had not committed.

In 1250 for the first time blood was shed in Saragossa. It caused a new problem: "the disputations", polemics to defend Judaism from Christianity. Spanish opinion was moved by a series of such polemics and Jews began to analyze and reconsider their religion to find the reasons for their situation.

Dominican monks who had been trained in militant evangelization were at the forefront of the disputes that were rarely even sided because Christians could, with full freedom, abuse Jews while these could not openly express their opinions. Anything that was said against Christianity was considered blasphemous. Judges were usually representatives either of the Church or the king. The proceedings were always humiliating for Jews because they ended up by arguing that salvation could only be reached by embracing the Christian faith.[13]

In this climate of insecurity for Jews a new philosophy of life and its interpretation began developing. The Cabbalah, a mystic interpretation of the Talmud transplanted in the 13th century from Provence to Gerona, appeared.

Cabbalah comes from the Hebrew word that means to receive, that is, it refers to receiving tradition. This doctrine was at the beginning transmitted orally but in secret, and later condensed in two books: the *Book of Creation (Yetzirah)* and the *Book of Splendor (Zohar)*. The *Zohar* is the most important literary work of the Cabbala. Its inspiration comes from Maimonides' *Guide of the Perplexed.*[14]

The most prominent work of theosophy and interpretation of the Cabbalah and the Zohar were written by the Spaniard Moses of Leon in the 13th century.

Among the many causes of the historic exile of the Jewish people, which is the spiritual one according to the Cabbalah, are due to disturbances and

---

[13] Bamberger, Bernard J. *The Story of Judaism,* New York, Schoken Books, 1971, p. 183.

[14] The Zohar is the most important literary work established from 1300 to 1800 but its influence ceased being so decisive when Jewish Enlightenment appeared in the 18th century.

failures in the cosmic harmony that serves as a concrete symbol. Only through individual efforts can mystic man, by himself, aspire to be redeemed.

In these Spanish circles, belief in the mystic nature of the Messiah first appeared. It would be created by special activity of the Creator and its origin would serve to raise its powers of seizure over all the angels.

Exile was considered not merely a test and punishment but also as a mission. "The Messiah would not arrive until the universe were complete and beyond all evil."[15]

In Judaism, from the very beginning, Messianic theories were of catastrophic origin. This means that the venerated Messiah would arrive after a great catastrophe.

Because of the forced conversions that were then occurring, the efforts of Spanish Cabbalists led towards a new understanding of Judaism. They reexamined Jewish life, the Ten Commandments, the world of the *Halakha* or Law, penetrating the mysteries of the Bible, human labor in the world and the relationship of man with God.

The Cabbalah became for the studious the object of special mystic meditations. Spaniards, whether Jewish or Christian, became mystics.

Jews penetrated deeper and deeper into Cabbalah and its mysteries for the path that would lead faster to God. Various new observances appeared at the time, such as fasting on moon days, nocturnal study at Pentecost and at the beginning of every month and the seventh day of Passover. Special solemnities surrounded the Sabbath when the union of man and God was expected.

The attitude of Christian monarchs towards Jews was never defined. Alfonso XI banned any usury by Jews, but he let them continue residing in his reign.

---

[15] Scholem, Gershom, *The Messianic Idea in Judaism,* New York, Schoken Books, 1972, p. 13.

His successor, Pedro the Cruel (1350-1369), recalled the Jews to his court and he took Samuel b. Meir Halevy Abulafia as chief treasurer, granting him a permit to build a synagogue in Toledo in 1357.

During the rule of Jaime II (1291-1327), the Inquisition entered the scene showing special interest in Jews, but the king responded that their presence was a question of State and not the Church. Many of the Jews who had been expelled from France were again allowed entrance into Spain in 1306.

Bloodshed began for the Jews when the Black Death began affecting some of the kingdoms in which Jews lived.

At that time, Barcelona established a Council of 30 people, selected among the most noted in the community (judges, administrators, physicians, etc.) who had the power to collect taxes.

By being close to the court, Hasdai Crescas, born in Barcelona, became the most venerated Jew in Spanish Jewry. According to Crescas, there was no other reason beyond revelation and faith: these should be the cornerstones of Jewish religious life.

One of the main concerns of the communities referred to the morals of its members. So they formed the Berurei Averah, institution unique in its type in medieval Spain formed by noted members that took care of the religious life of their communities.

Very soon, the face of Spanish Jewry changed radically. In 1378, the dean of Ecija, Ferrant Martínez, launched a violent campaign against Jews, asking for the destruction of 23 local synagogues. When the archbishop died in 1390, Ferrant became virtual leader of the diocese using his position to intensify an anti-Jewish crusade, stating that not even the monarchy would oppose an attack. Upon the death of King John I of Castile in 1390, the crown was vested on a minor who did not dare or knew how to stand against the preacher's calls.

Disturbances began in Seville on June 4, 1391. The doors of the Jewish quarter were put to fire and many died. Synagogues were converted into churches and the Christians started to inhabit former Jewish homes.

The attacks continued in Madrid, Cuenca, Burgos and Cordoba; the monarchs made efforts to protect the Jews to no avail. Violence broke loose in Aragon, the community in Valencia was destroyed and more than 250 Jews were slain; a few managed to escape. In the Balearic Islands more than 300 people were brutally murdered and those who tried to flee were forced to convert or die.

More than 400 Jews were killed in Barcelona in August and the same number in Gerona. The Jews of Tortosa, where a famous disputation had taken place, were forced to convert. Practically all the communities in Aragon were destroyed by the masses. The Jews who managed to stay alive and convert had their property stolen or confiscated.

Jews began to alter their ways, they ceased being active, productive, enterprising: "…. with the sad experience that word of their wealth was a constant incentive for popular greed and with the unfounded suspicion that they would attract about their heritage and movable assets, by keeping their envied treasures in the earth's entrails; they preferred so doing and dying in the sterility of inaction than being as before, useful to a society and a State that had so rudely expelled them from their midst."[16]

Matters went back to an apparent normality, although nobody in Spain raised a protest. The great aljamas of Barcelona, Valencia and Mallorca were extinguished.

Free cultural exchange came to an end. The banner of those who since the 15th century had been adamant about the unity of Christian Spain now had one sole religion, State and culture in the spirit of the dominating Church.

In 1391 John I ordered "new Christians" to live segregated from Jews. The apparently normal situation changed for Crypto-Jews because they

---

[16] Amador de los Ríos, *op .cit.,* Vol. II, p.7.

began to rethink their ancestral beliefs and about how they had committed an offense against Judaism. Little by little they found the way to return to their faith, their Judaism, whether totally or partially. Because conversions had been made massively, they remained a separate group, easy to identify, always marked by old Christians.

Many names were used to designate them: that of converts was surely the most common and the one that has remained. Discrepancies abound about the origin of other words used to call those newly converted: one of them is "marrano". Poliakov refers to it as "deriving from the Castilian word marrano or pig that comes from the Arabic mahram that means forbidden".[17] Nicolás López Martínez considers the word an insult.[18]

In the 16th and 17th centuries convert was anybody who had an infidel as ancestor, even if very remotely. In the last third of the 15th century time could go back two or three generations, because infidelity had begun counting more or less in 1391. The appellation of "new Christian" began to be used as opposed to old Christians or "lindos".[19] At the end of the 15th century writings with the title of "alboraiques or alboraicos" sometimes appeared as applied to converts.[20] The curious book *Libro del Alboraique,* disclosed by the Jewish investigator Isidoro Loeb, offers an interesting tale of the origin of the name and its meaning.

The introduction to the book refers to the reason for the name:

"In the town of Erena, of the province of Leon, the name was given to new Judaizers, we should know that converts who became Christians now and sixty or more years ago, and the war that occurred in all of Spain in death by the sword, we should know about the destruction in the aljamas of the Jews, and those

---

[17] Poliakov, León, *Histoire de L'antisemitisme de Mahomet aux Marranes,* Paris, Calmann-Levy, 1961, Collection Liberté de l'esprit, p. 218.
[18] López Martínez, Nicolás, *Los Judaizantes Castellanos y la Inquisición en Tiempos de Isabel la Católica,* Burgos, 1954, 0. 53.
[19] We consider "new Christian" one who really accepted Catholicism.
[20] Roth, Cecil, *Historia de los Marranos,* Buenos Aires, Editorial Israel, 1941, p. 33.

that remained alive in the most part were baptized by force and they took as their name the Hebrew Anuzim, that means forced. And if somebody became Christian called Mesumad that in Hebrew means returner who returns to Christianity. And if somebody of this lineage arrives where there is bad blood, they ask are you anuz, forced Christian or mesuma, Christian by desire. If he answers anuz, they honor him and give him presents, but if he says mesumad, total silence greets him just as those that returned; others in this Andalusia and Spain who are Christian anuzim, more I cannot do because that is in the name, good for labors, keeping Sabbath and other Jewish ceremonies, praying in Jewish books although they are circumcised just like Moors and have Sabbath like Jews, and just the name of Christians and they are not Moors, nor Jews, nor Christians, although by desire Jews, but they do not keep the Talmud nor all the Jewish ceremonies, even less Christian law. And this was the reason that such a vituperation was put on their name it is better that they are called Alboraicos all of them and one is an Alboraico.

And as I was looking for this name in the old and new law and in the commentaries and didn't find it, but I found it in the Coran...."[21]

These forced Christians or anuzim remained inwardly faithful to their religion and kept it under wraps with great zeal.

Converts would usually perform their religious rites in total secrecy without letting their family and underage children find out. In time, these converts became distant from non-converted Jews because their rites were kept secret. After the expulsion in 1492, many of these Crypto-Jews had no way of keeping in contact with Judaism and not having recourse to the Law

---

[21] López Martínez, *op. cit.* p. 391 (documentary appendix). ,

and the Talmud they began to blend all kinds of traditions the led them to become a very special group. Many of the ceremonies they held were not really Jewish anymore because many traits had been taken from Christianity.

In Spanish society in which the influence of these strange elements became more and more prevalent, a deep mistrust mixed with fear began to appear. People who had no tolerance whatsoever towards Judaism were suspected of being in sympathy with it. There was a feeling that there were hidden paths of "inside enemies" of the Church in every corner.

Neither the Church nor the State created conditions of any kind to absorb these converts. They continued living in their old sectors and performing the same trades. The community of converts little by little began to segregate itself, sometimes for security and others because both the Jewish and the Christian communities shunned them. It was a fringe group, neither Jewish nor Spanish.

The situation in those days seemed deplorable; whatever ailed the country, under population, misery, hunger, desperation, everything was blamed on converts. The populace felt that Jews had swindled them once so their ire had been launched trying to stop that injustice; now it turned out that the network of tax collectors, customs agents, court officers, etc. that had "crushed them financially, were not Jewish in name but just as Jewish in fact, since they continued oppressing them more and more with the same former methods. They had been Jews, now they were converts."[22]

The first serious disturbance occurred in Toledo, capital of Castile, in 1449 because of a fight for public positions. This outburst was not religious, but rather socio-economic. Chancellor Alvaro de Luna demanded from the citizens an extraordinary contribution of a million maravedis to protect the border, but the Toledan Council refused to pay. Then the tax collectors, "new Christians" by origin, were ordered to force people to pay. As soon as they

---

[22] *Ibidem,* p. 56.

began the task, the citizens burned down the house of the wealthy tax collector continuing with the homes of other new Christians.

After the turmoil in Toledo many innocent people were blamed, among them fourteen converts who were not directly connected. Because converts were considered infidels that was reason enough to be processed. They were accused of occupying forbidden positions, of "infiltrating these posts" that should be given to pure Christians. This situation gave rise to a number of publications referring to the problem of converts. In 1460, a Franciscan monk, Alonso de Espina, wrote a book in which he asked for drastic measures to be taken against converts. This book entitled *Fortaliquim Liqui*, or in defense of faith, is a handbook for those who wanted to eradicate converts whether from Spain or elsewhere.[23] The book was later used as a guide by inquisitors. It gives a faithful description of converts of the time, about circumcision and the way of teaching children Jewish rites.

This monk may be considered precursor of the Spanish Inquisition. Others, such as Alvaro de Oropeza and Diego Hurtado de Mendoza, requested an integral education for converts and demanded an inquisition to extirpate all loyalty to Judaism.

The question of converts produced a division in Spanish society. Traditional Spaniards totally avoided new Christians. They would not accept them within their families and would not allow them to have any public positions. More open groups, of which new Christians formed a large part, tried very hard to erase the separation between Christian Spaniards and the assimilated descendants of baptized Jews.

At that moment the term called "blood purity" came into being. It meant seeking for no trace of Judaism among one's ancestors, obsession that would appear both in Spain and Portugal in the 15th century based on the desire of a mystic society for no taint as the most important matter in being a Christian.

---

[23] The name means "Strengthening the Faith against Jews, Saracens and Other Enemies of the Christian Religion"

This fixation afflicted Spain as well as America up to the 19th century. The statutes about blood purity were established in Spain in the 16th century and were led against Christians who descended from Moors or Jews, particularly the latter. Churches and cathedrals reserved the right to ban entrance to Christians who descended from Jews. Everyone feared that they would be found to have the slightest hint of Jewish blood and thus of being impure. This situation lent itself to false testimonies, fake documents, and blackmail.

Various Christian kings made efforts to unite their territories and expand their personal power. But both nobles and the urban middle class opposed them.

Tens of thousands of people, particularly high-class Jews, had accepted being baptized. Spanish clergy called for everybody who had been baptized to become a good Christian.

Some of those Jews decided to look for new places to live and abandoned the country searching for lands where they could freely serve the God of Israel. But most new Christians continued to hope for a change of luck, waiting for the day when they could go back to Judaism within the borders of their own country.

All during the 15th century, the Church was concerned about a newly created problem, the converts. It tried to talk to the Jewish communities that helped these Crypto-Jews so as to punish anyone who helped them or to reveal the name of new Christian infidels, but this was obviously almost impossible to achieve.

In the meanwhile, discontent was increasing in other aspects. Anybody would have thought that Christians who had been clamoring to convert Jews would be satisfied and would receive them gladly. But exactly the opposite happened: new Christians were not accepted among "old" ones.

The clergy found only one solution to the problem of infidel Christians. Theirs was the path of terror and force. Little by little a number of friars began to request introduction of the Inquisition. The civil government was against it because it acted on its own without taking into account the legally established system of the country. To begin with, punishment by the Inquisition meant confiscation of assets which enriched the Holy Office stripping the royal treasury of taxes.

Many opposed the establishment of the Holy Office, not just the converts who viewed it with horror, including kings and some bishops. But these objections were refuted by many Christians willing to exterminate heresy, to free themselves from the converts, eagerness of the aristocracy to eliminate competition or at least throw suspicion upon competent rivals and the ambition of King Ferdinand to increase the royal treasure if he could stop confiscations.

In 1480, a considerable number of "new Christians" were found celebrating the Jewish ceremony of the Passover supper. Queen Isabella of Castile was terribly impressed upon hearing of this incident so she decided to accept establishment of the Inquisition in her domain. The Pope agreed.

A Code of terror was published in 1488 called "Instructions" to correct inquisitorial excesses that were about to canonize them with the solemnity and investiture of the law and leave the oppressed defenseless.

When Ferdinand and Isabella acceded to the throne, the Jewish situation worsened noticeably.

In 1480, the queen decided to make a partial experiment seemingly to replace the Inquisition. Since Andalusia was the province with the greatest number of Jews, she ordered the expulsion of all those who had not accepted Christianity and threatened any others who attempted to settle there with the death penalty.

Jews continued appearing in the diplomatic service of the Catholic Monarchs and they were treated as valuable and necessary officers while their utter ruin was being contemplated. The treasury and administration of the court of Ferdinand the Catholic was made up mainly by converts. Among these we find the families of Santangel, Sánchez and Caballería. These were some of the people who were persecuted by the Inquisition for resisting establishment of that sinister tribunal in Aragon which went against all rights and freedoms of the kingdom.

Some authors state that Ferdinand's benevolence towards Jews was because of his Jewish ancestry. Américo Castro explains it this way: "John II of Aragon's second wife, Juana Henríquez, was daughter of a Castilian admiral. Her son, Ferdinand the Catholic, was Jewish on his mother's side."[24]

The war against the Moors in Granada that Ferdinand had initiated required the effort of all the financial energy of the country. By ironic fate, Rabbi Isaac Abrabanel had to help the Spaniards with his financial genius to undertake a feat that had fatal results for Spanish Jewry.

The last war against the Moors lasted ten years. In 1487, Malaga fell and the Spaniards took several hundred Jewish prisoners there. On January 2, 1492, Ferdinand and Isabella entered Granada with great solemnity. Now, the reconquest was complete.

The aspiration of generations had finally been concluded. The last bastion of Islam had been defeated on that day of 1492 after enduring seven hundred seventy eight years in the Iberian Peninsula.

In 1490, a convert named Benito García was detained and a Christian host was found in his possession. He was tortured until he confessed some alleged crimes attributed to him and he mentioned some friends five of whom were converts and one Jew. They were accused of having crucified, extracting the blood and the heart of a Christian boy in the city of Guardia. This, according to the inquisitors, had been made through a general conspiracy scheme of all the Jewish communities. There had never been any concrete proof because nobody ever found the supposed body of the murdered child.

In the words of Benito García, the convert, we may see the drama of such people when he said: "I was born Jewish and was baptized 40 years ago, but

---

[24] Castro, *op. cit.* P. 498.

a short time ago I came to see the truth: Christianity seemed to me a great comedy of paganism and in my heart I returned to Judaism. The terrible Autos-da-fe of the Inquisition filled my heart with pity for the victims and hate for the executioner. I began to hate Christianity. If a baptized Jew is the anti-Christ, an inquisitor is a worse one. I practice Judaism in secret and go to Church only when I can't help going. I don't keep Christian festivities, I eat meat in Holy Week and I go to confession with the priest to keep appearances. I comply with all Jewish commandments, like resting on the Sabbath, eating and drinking what is kosher (Jewish ritual food). I don't eat on Jewish fast days and even in jail I say my Jewish prayers. I receive my scourges meekly because I deserve them; they are the punishment for having made my parents suffer when I adopted the Christian religion and by leading my children to Church. Now I have only one desire: for my children to abandon this false religion and become Jews. When I leave this jail I will go to Palestine and convince others to do the same."[25]

The accused were put to the stake. The excited Christian population of Avila was ready to destroy the whole Jewish community. The Jews were forced to ask the king for mercy, to beseech him to protect them from death. This happened two months before Granada fell to the Spaniards.

Exactly three months after their victory, Isabella and Ferdinand signed in Avila the "General Edict of Expulsion" of the Jews of Aragon and Castile on March 31, 1492.

The kingdom was going through bad times, because good order in a nation cannot be based exclusively on beliefs, passions, and desires.

When the Catholic Monarchs were preparing the Edict of Expulsion, it is said that the document was edited by a court convert; several wise statesmen and rabbis tried to prevent such a tragedy, offering 300,000 gold ducats for the war against the Moors.

---

[25] Dubnow, *op. cit.* Vol. V, p. 330..

The Edict of Expulsion, signed in March of 1492, gave the Jewish population a term up to July 31 to either embrace the Catholic faith or else leave the country. During this interval, many Jews remained under royal protection. They were allowed to sell their goods and take some assets with them, except for gold and silver.

The Spain of the Catholic Monarchs had reached a religious aspect that it had not had at the beginning. It did not take part in the Crusades because it had its own inside struggle against infidels. The energy accumulated by this and the final success of the enterprise gave the Spanish people the feeling of having "a mission to conclude on earth", that of dominating the enemies of God as the executor arm of His designs. Thus, the united policy was made under the sign of religious unity, after defeating the Moors and expelling the Jews."[26]

Américo Castro very accurately comments: "Towards the end of the 15th century the Spanish population believed that the Catholic Monarchs had been sent by God to restore happiness on earth and to finish with the tyranny of the powerful. Some Renaissance thinkers wrote utopias, but the Spaniards gave their blood for such dreams in more than one occasion, thus erasing the border between the possible, the real and the imaginary.[27]

"Juan López de Palacios, eminent jurist of the Catholic court, recognized that infidels may have wars bestowed on them when they don't recognize the authority of the Church, prevent propagation of the faith, harass Christians, blaspheme or commit crimes of lese majesty."[28]

About the expulsion of the Jews, Lacalle indicates: The expulsion cannot be understood in the pagan world in which we live. It would have no justification in a world of perfect application of the evangelic doctrine, but

---

[26] Jiménez Rueda, Julio, *Historia de la Cultura en México. El Virreinato,* Mexico, Editorial Cultura, 1960, p. 14.

[27] Castro, *España en su Historia, Cristianos, Moros y Judíos,* Buenos Aires, (s.e.), 1948, p. 101.

[28] Jiménez Rueda, *op. cit.,* p. 20.

the deeply religious Spain of the 15th century did not find it difficult to see itself as a faithful interpreter of the message of the Sermon of the Mount. The religious delirium – under a military backdrop, a mystic and ascetical Spain – made the Christian Spaniards believe that they were THE PEOPLE FOR GOD. In this aspect they could not but be jealous of THE PEOPLE OF GOD."[29]

Nicolás López Martínez considers that political unity could only be had with religious unity. If Catholicism was endangered in Castile, its political being was also at risk.

Prescott, in his history of the Catholic Monarchs, says that it was "the fanatic populace, often stimulated by the no less fanatical clergy and perhaps also by the numerous debtors of Jews who saw this as a very expeditious measure to save their debts, the ones that so ferociously attacked this unfortunate people in Castile and Aragon…"[30]

The Edict of 1492 meant for the Jew absence from home and country, physical and mental suffering and death for those who were sick, very old or too young to undertake this trip. The mere thought of leaving the peninsula and never coming back was an absolute tragedy.

The first day of August was the term fixed to leave Spain, but the monarchs granted up to the second day to the last groups.

To sell all the assets and close off one's business, those expelled were given such a brief time that land had to be sold at very low prices. A house was traded for a donkey, a vineyard for some yards of material, a great part of the houses was left unsold.

The terror and affliction of the exodus were increased in great proportion by an Edict issued in April by Juan de la Torquemada, Inquisitor General,

---

[29] Lacalle, José María, *Los Judíos Españoles,* Barcelona, Sayma Ediciones, 1964, p. 20.
[30] Prescott, W.H., *Historia del Reinado de los Reyes Católicos, Don Fernando y Doña Isabel,* Vol. I, México, 1854, p. 99.

forbidding Christians to keep any communication, provide food, housing or help Jews in any way whatsoever after August 9.

When Jews reached some ports to embark, they found out that there was an export duty of two ducats per person, which they had to pay from their impoverished pockets. Those that had not left at the time fixed for exit had their property confiscated.

There is no way of knowing exactly how many Jews left Spain in 1492. Baer calculates that 35,000 families were expelled from Spain.[31]

"On the first day of August of 5252 of the creation (computed by Jewish writers), three hundred thousand people left Spain, land where their ancestors had lived for two thousand years."[32] Amador refers to "four hundred forty thousand souls".

Many converted and remained there, but many more left, a great majority strengthened by the Rabbis who helped them remain true to their beliefs.

Endless suffering became the lot of the Jews who left Spain; hunger, disease and death went with them at every moment. Spain expelled hundreds of thousands of modest and cultivated citizens. "This way, Spain established religious unity, but at the same time it gave the first step towards its economic and cultural decay. By expelling the Jews, it lost its active industrious class that had helped prepare the natural wealth of the country. The "marranos" who remained in Spain continued developing the economic activities of the Jews and, in the next century, generated a vast commercial network with the new Spanish colonies in America; but also in the 16th century the marranos began to flee from the country of the Inquisition and this dealt the final blow to Spain's well being after the disaster of the expulsion of Jews".[33]

---

[31] Baer, Fritz, *Die Juden in Chrsitlichen Spanien,* Farnborough Gregg, 1970, pp. 652-653.
[32] Amador, *op. cit.,* Vol.II, pp. 217-218.
[33] Dubnow, *op. cit.* Vol. V, p. 334.

The aristocracy of many European and American cities became the richer by these people and their descendants. In Spain, Jews and converts had headed an intellectual movement, both literary and scientific.

Most of the people expelled went to Portugal where fully one fourth of the population was of Jewish origin, according to Professor Beinart.[34] They lived there until 1506 at which time they were allowed to leave. Beginning at that moment, they began to return in secret to Spain, to their land of origin, establishing an intensive and constant communication through the border. People who lived in permanent seesaw from Spain to Portugal and from Portugal to Spain were usually members of the same family; some lived in one country and others in the next one, but they all spoke both Castilian and Portuguese.

The discovery, conquest and colonization of America opened to these Sephardim a wide field of action and immense territories where they could hide their Judaism and from the borders of Portugal they began moving to Andalusian cities and ports, mainly towards Seville and from there to America.[35]

---

[34] Beinart, Haim, *"La Sociedad Hispano-Judía"*, conference quoted.
[35] Del Hoyo, Eugenio, *Historia del Nuevo Reino de León (1577-1723),* 2 vols. Monterrey, 1972, Serie Historia, No. 13, pp. 202-203.

Coat of arms used by the Mexican Inquisition with the shield of the same Inquisition, the Spanish king's and that of Mexico City

CHAPTER II
IDENTITY

Judeo-Spanish Identity

1492 was a year of calamities for humanity as a whole but it was particularly so for the Jewish people. Columbus' discovery of the New World also marked the end of a flourishing center of Jewish creativity.

Although Spanish Judaism was already showing signs of spiritual and physical erosion that also evinced the marks of persecution and oppression, it was still the light of world Jewry. As an economic, influential, cultivated powerhouse of accumulated traditions and spiritual wealth, it kept unequaled supremacy. No wonder then that the expulsion of Jews from golden Iberia was such a catastrophe that shook every Jewish soul of the day and its echoes were felt for many centuries afterward.

Wandering from one port to another under degrading conditions, the Jew could raise his eyes with the rich imagery and poetic fantasies of the *Zohar* that helped him forget his hunger and humiliation.

Cabbalists, like most Jews, believed that utter redemption was just around the corner. In their expulsion from Spain they viewed the principle of "the Messiah's work", the beginning of those terrible disasters and afflictions that would conclude history and from which redemption would emerge.

That same Messianic spirit of hope of salvation, of the search for an "apocalyptic message" could be found not only among the Jews traveling to Palestine but also among the converts going towards the New World.

Converts were convinced that after great suffering and martyrdom, the Messiah would come to earth; thus, the majority accepted punishment from the Inquisition considering that they (the martyrs) were the instruments for achieving that dream.

When Ana López, wife of Diego López Regalón, was indicted for observing the Law of Moses in New Spain, she was accused of having expected the Messiah and of having fasted on the great day...[36]

After the expulsion two forces emerged to justify the Cabbalah and Messianic feelings. Jews began wondering about the reason for their sufferings, of the expulsion; what led to it? What were the problems of the Diaspora? etc. They sought for answers to all their doubts based on mysticism and its symbols. Among converts, the thought of redemption flourished at once. "It has been ordained that the king Messiah be clothed in marrano robes and he should walk among his fellow Jews and not be recognized. In other words it is ordained that he be a marrano just like I."[37]

The need for a Messiah went hand in hand with the feelings of Crypto-Jews and their mentality. They actually though they could be humanity's redeemers and used the story of Queen Esther, who originally did not tell the Persian king that she was Jewish but then revealed it and saved her people, as an example.

Being a convert was never an obstacle to return to the old religion, even less so now when their situation might help bring the Redeemer to earth. This doctrine of an apostate Messiah served to keep up the spirit of Crypto-Jews.

Because of their suffering and persecutions, Jewish way of life changed. Jews became more hermetic, more careful, less straightforward, more confused, situation that led them to become mystics.

"Mysticism, fear of gossip, quietism, Messianic pride, divinability and so many other facets of our Hispanic character, says Lacalle, are consequences of the mixture of Hispano-Jews and our ancestral fusion with converts.[38]

---

[36] Process against Ana López, wife of Diego López Regalón of Castelo Blanco, 1595, A.G.N.M., V. 155, file 2.
[37] Scholem, *op. cit.,* p. 43.
[38] Lacalle, *op. cit.,* p. 21.

Jewish Spaniards were conscious of their Spanish self; fifteen centuries had left their traces in their inner being. They felt that Spain was their homeland, the place where their grandparents and great grandparents had lived, where they had created and developed their intellect, a place of fond memories. The customs, habits, traditions, speech and behavior of the Spanish people would all remain within them.

Spaniards, whether Jewish, Christian or Moslem, felt a bond to one land, one past. They loved everything Spanish, the culture, the history.

Spanish Jews were Jewish and Spanish. The same way of life, Spanish culture rooted within Judaism, love for the land where they had been born, where their children had grown up and where their grandparents were buried. America appeared like a prize for their faith, their martyrdom, their suffering. Not only for them as Judaizers, but for every Spaniard and in this case the Jew was a Spaniard to the bottom of his heart.

CHAPTER III
NEW SPANISH JEWS

In Search for a New World

Colonization of America happened at a time of great spiritual dread, dread caused by the Renaissance ideas that transformed the concept that man had of the world and life in the Middle Ages. The American continent was a favorable land to find liberty. A number of diverse and heterogeneous kinds of people whose purpose was very varied arrived there.

The Spaniards who came from the Old World brought along the religious fear that was characteristic of those times. Faced with the dogmatic authority of the Church, they sought free inquiry with all its consequences.

During the second half of the 16th century, Europe was going through one of the most critical moments of humanity. Spain was the foremost power in the world and its discoveries had added an extension never dreamed of by anyone as it undertook to achieve the unity of the European world. Charles V, Lord of the Holy Roman Empire, reigned. His eyes viewed Europe more than America, because he could barely understand those who were expanding his territory in the New World.

A number of issues arose among the three great European powers: Spain under Charles V, France under Francis I and England with Henry VIII. Charles V became the leader of Catholicism against Protestant Reformation.

The situation of converts became gradually more and more difficult. It was no longer easy to continue practicing Judaism. The tribunal of the

Inquisition kept close watch day and night so converts believed that perhaps in the New World they might be more distant from danger.

Just like Christian Spaniards, converts hoped that honor and nobility would lead to salvation. They identified with the Messiah through language and many traditions; they were convinced that they were the intermediaries between the divinity and humans so the Messiah would arrive and for that they were ready to face any risk. They knew that in New Spain there would be many obstacles, which would only be divine proof that redemption was about to come.

Spaniards viewed America as the prize for their faith, reward for having achieved the reconquest of the fatherland from the hands of infidels, with an obligation for taking the divine word to the new lands. Converts just as Spaniards viewed America as their redemption, as the longed for land where happiness would reign.

History of the Discoveries

The discovery of America by Columbus can be considered as the culmination of a prolonged historic and scientific evolution in which Jews were very prominent. Because Jews and converts were in such pressing circumstances in the peninsula, many of them were more apt to join the new ventures towards unknown destinies.

The role of both Jews and converts in the discovery of the new continent was remarkable. Their participation in the discovery of the Indies and their colonization and development (although very obvious in the pages of history told by eminent historians of those days) is mostly unknown. The first great convert we find in America is Columbus himself. Although prevailing opinion considers Columbus as Genoan, we believe we must pause and discuss the origin of this character.

Ricardo Albanés, in his work *Los Judíos a Través de los Siglos,* says, referring to Columbus: "His primitive name was Cristóforo Colombi, he was a baptized Jew."[39]

Werner Sombart tends to believe that Columbus was Jewish according to the facts quoted by Celso García de la Riega before the Madrid Geographic Society and in what refers to Jewish participation in his travels. He also explains and stresses one of Columbus' reasons to set out on his journey: "He was saturated by a Messianic spirit and he believed he had been called to rebuild Jerusalem."[40]

The historian Salvador de Madariaga, one of the biographers of the great navigator, indicates: "Columbus' parents, named Colom, came from Catalonia and were probably fugitive Marranos, among the many who went to Italy before 1492. We know that many marrano families settled in Genoa, Venice and other important Italian cities from fear of inquisitorial persecution, but because heretic assets were confiscated and divided by the Church and the Crown, temptation was too great and in Italy they could easily pass as Christians. But the truth is, and it is not mere coincidence, that the main sponsors and collaborators of Columbus were Sephardim and sons of Sephardim."[41]

It is also significant that Columbus appears, in some portraits of his time, with his hand on his breast as is traditional among Jews, that is, the index and small finger separated by the united middle and second finger. This gesture has a ritual and liturgical meaning. Columbus himself never said in any authentic document that he was Genoan.

---

[39] Albanés, Ricardo, *Los Judíos a Través de los Siglos, Historia, Religión, Psicología y Política de Israel,* México, 1939, p. 258.

[40] Sombart, Werner, *op. cit., apud.* in Albanés, *op. cit.,* p. 267.

[41] Estrugo, José M., *Los Sefardíes,* La Habana, 1958, Editorial Lex, p. 22. Descendants of those expelled from Spain and Portugal who refused to convert to Catholicism and the "marranos" and converts who remained there and who later fled to the East and other places in the world are called Sephardim.

In Fernando Columbus' biography of his father, he quotes words of his father writing to Prince John's housekeeper where he refers very enigmatically to his family: "I am not the first admiral of my family, whatever name you use, and David too, very wise king, was shepherd and later became king of Jerusalem. I am a servant of that same Lord that set David in that State."[42]

On one hand, this quote has a reference to another admiral in the family and, on the other, he recognizes his humble origin and alludes to Jewish history.

It is interesting that Columbus began his first log with a letter to the Catholic Monarchs that begins as follows: "So, after having thrown out all the Jews from your kingdoms and dominions, in the same month of January (that should be March) your Majesties sent me with enough of an army to go to those areas of the Indies; and for this you gave a number of mercies and ennobled me so that hereon I would be called Don and be Great Admiral of the Oceans and Viceroy and perpetual Governor of all the islands and the mainland."[43]

The fact that Columbus should mention as memorable date, not the conquest of Granada that took place that same year, or any other historic event but rather the expulsion of Jews, gives us a clue that this occurrence was very high in his mind.

Maurice David in his book *Who was Columbus?* refers to some mysterious signs appearing on the left-hand side of private letters that could be abbreviations of Hebrew lettering meaning: "With the help of God."[44]

The enigmatic seven letters that Columbus sets before his signature would be composed, according to the usual interpretation, of the following: "God,

---

[42] E.J.C., Vol. III, p. 90.

[43] *Ibidem.*

[44] David, Maurice, *¿Quién era Colón?, apud.* In E.J.C., *op. cit.,* Vol. III, p. 900.

Lord God, God full of Mercy that forgives all iniquity, transgressions and sin."

From this, we can infer that Columbus was not only son of converts, but Crypto-Jew, because this Hebrew phrase is a convert prayer asking divine forgiveness for having abandoned the faith of his ancestors.

The valuable assistance that America's discoverer had from many Jewish people and sages while preparing his extraordinary feat are undeniable. Among the Jews who helped Columbus was Abraham Zacuto, professor at the University of Salamanca, who provided the maps (he also used the nautical compass of Spanish and Portuguese Jews); Diego de Deza, bishop and professor of the same university, originally from Pontevedra and new Christian; Abraham Senior and Isaac Abrabanel, influential financiers and businessmen in the great court; Luis de Santangel, king's confidant; Gabriel Sánchez, Royal treasurer and Juan Cabrero. All these were sons of converts and open backers of Columbus.

Fernando Columbus states that Luis de Santangel gave the first steps to convince the Spanish Monarchs to finance Columbus' expedition. The queen thanked him and offered to sell her jewels to help the project but he refused her gesture.

The privileges granted to Columbus were put in writing by the State Secretary of Aragon, son of a Jewish mother, who 18 days earlier had also edited the Decree of Expulsion.

A circumstance that seems to have delayed Columbus' voyage was the huge exodus of Spanish Jews. Originally, the date for any non-baptized person to leave was on July 31. When the authorities realized this was impossible to perform, the last date was set for August 2.

The wealthiest Jews hired ships in Spanish ports and then proceeded to fill them up with their people and belongings. Perhaps the ship owners of Palos and Moguer thought they might make more money with fewer risks from the deported oppressed Jews than hiring out their caravels to Columbus.

Maybe this explains the fact that Columbus had to be satisfied with the Santa Maria that was not in the best of conditions.

The monarchs desired that the New World would have only Spaniards of Christian ancestors, of pure blood three generations back. They did not want America to be contaminated by Jewish or Moorish blood and thus their Decrees and Edicts forbade entrance to the Indies to any convert.

Forbidden entrance to New Spain

Latin America attracted a great number of New Christians. The advantage of those territories was that they offered converts a familiar culture and the possibility of some contact with the "Motherland". For new Christians who wanted to live as Catholics, the distance that separated them from the peninsula and the scarcity of settlers enabled them to erase their Jewish origin and to keep their blood impurity secret. The same factors also helped those who wanted to keep their Jewish rites alive.

Ever since the discovery of America, the right to immigrate to the New World was reserved for Catholic Spaniards, except for a brief interlude under the reign of Emperor Charles V (1516-1556). Preparing false permits became a profession and when sanctions became more severe, price only increased for those papers together with the development of more ingenious ways to evade the law by both sellers and buyers. Jews and Moors, together with foreigners, managed to get there without a permit. The two types of people who were banned entry from Castile to the Indies were converts, children and grandchildren of converts and foreigners which included Portuguese.

Ricardo Albanés, in his book *Los Judíos a Través de los Siglos,* mentions a great number of converts who were living in Mexico City and environs in the 16th century; his figure is of 300 people.

Many Portuguese who left Portugal for Spanish America, whether going through Castile or not, were descendants of Jewish converts. Lured by earnings from the colonial economy, they fled from an environment hostile to *cristaos novos,* seeking for a supposedly freer one, less dominated by discrimination and suspicious inquisitors. Inquisition processes against Jews allow us to see to what point the Portuguese element coincided in America's population with new Christians in the 16th century.

Beginning in 1580, long after the discovery, there was an authentic exodus of real or pretended converts to New Spain, both from the Iberian Peninsula or Portugal. Every single boat brought converts to the New World. Bans to the entry of converts began in 1501 and they would be repeated throughout the colonial era. However, the first ten years went by without any migratory restrictions.

The decree stated that only subjects of the Crown of Castile were authorized to go to the Indies and trade in those territories. Beginning in 1596, other Spaniards managed to have the same rights as Castilians, but strict prohibitions persisted for foreigners.

The Legal Doctrine did not completely close off access to foreigners into the Indies. "The legal incapacity that derived from their condition as foreigners could be remedied also legally, by obtaining a Royal Bill of Naturalization. Requirements changed according to the times. At the first moment, to get one it was enough to have lived for ten years in an open house and to be married with a woman born in the kingdom of Castile."[45]

Abuse was rampant but by falsifying the information required, a great number of foreigners were easily able to enter.

Naturalization was not the only legal way to allow foreigners to inhabit the newly discovered areas. The need to promote the occupation of "certain trades" and mechanical professions in the Indies made the Spanish government allow entry of some foreigners who were well versed in them. They had to pass an ability test and present bail which guaranteed that they

---

[45] Capdequi Ots, J.M., *El Estado Español en las Indias,* 4th Ed., Mexico, Fondo de Cultura Económica, 1956, p. 21.

would continue performing the trades to which they had accredited efficiency.

Besides, there was always the possibility of an "individual license" obtained by means of some prominent title. Those foreigners who had entered covertly could usually compose or pay some amount to obtain a permit that would allow them to continue living in the Indies. These foreigners composed files can be "solved with lesser or greater criterion, according to the needs of the Treasury".

At the time of Philip II, the practice already established in Spain was that council functions and those requiring writing – clerks and actuaries of municipalities and audiences – were to be sold at public auction granting them to the highest bidder. There was the case of a convert called Diego de Ocaña, office clerk, who took advantage of this situation during the first years of the colony and was accused of Judaizing. Bernal Díaz del Castillo refers to an Edict that indicated: "And after their having published that all those who came from Jewish or Moorish lineage, that had been burned or worn a sambenito (penitent garment) of the Holy Inquisition, in fourth degree or their parents or those who within six months had left New Spain, under pain of losing half their assets and in that time would accuse, that they accused one another and informed what they did and did not leave New Spain but only two of them; one was a merchant in Veracruz and the other clerk in Mexico."[46]

Bernal also refers to said Judaizer as a person who walked about the city wearing "caftan and bonnet", the type of attire used by Jews in Poland or Lithuania from the 17th to the 20th century. No explanation has ever been found for such behavior.

Emperor Charles V and the prince in their Ordinances dictated a Decree in Valladolid on September 15, 1522 that forbade entrance to the Indies to

---

[46] Díaz del Castillo, Bernal, *Historia Verdadera de la Conquista de la Nueva España,* México, Editorial Porrúa, 1960, p. 491.

newly converted Jews, "and these dispositions were included in the Compilation of Laws of the Indies, Law 15 title XXVI book IX, that says to the letter: no new convert to our Holy Catholic Faith from Moor or Jew, nor his children can go to the Indies without our express license."

Law 24 title V book VII says: "With great diligence do inquire and try to know the viceroys, audiences, governors and justices, that slaves or Berber slaves or freemen newly converted from Moors or children of Jews, residing in the Indies or anywhere and throw out from there those found, sending them to these kingdoms in the first boats arriving and in no case to remain in those provinces."

As late as the 19th century there was still "an order neither to allow Jews on land nor to go inside any of the Spanish dominions."

The great migratory currents brought by the discovery of America caused numberless abuses and corruption that violated the efficacy of legal precepts that were continually being defined and sanctioned so it became necessary for legislators to react before the danger and release a huge number of Royal Decrees and other dispositions that pursued in every possible way compliance of such orders. Thus, one said: "women to be forced to give information about purity as well as men and not to let any of them enter without express license." This Decree was dated 1554.

In the legislation of the Indies heads of family were allowed to leave towards the new lands with their daughters or wives; it said, "that no married man may go to those territories without being accompanied by his wife."[47]

The ban for "new Christians" of going to America remained permanently in force and adequate measures were installed, demanding special requirements for disembarking in any port of the American continent that belonged to the Spanish crown. A license issued by the House of Contracts was required which requested the necessary information from the places of origin that would state blood purity, neighborhood and state, etc. "The

---

[47] Capdequi, *op. cit.,* p. 96.

obligation of accountants and overseers of the fleet of making diligences about the immigrants that go in each vessel and arrest those traveling without it; the duty incumbent to governors and commissaries of the ports touched by fleets arriving in the New World of disallowing disembarkation of those not having fulfilled the previous formality."[48]

Many tried to enroll in the retinue of some nobleman who was leaving because he could get a license for himself and his servants.

There were many who went to Africa towards the possessions of the Portuguese crown to purchase Negroes whom they would sell in the Spanish colonies. After several trial journeys they would settle in the colonies with the "surreptitious collaboration of the authorities, naturally losing bail deposited as guarantee that far from remaining in America they would go back to Spain."[49]

The slave trade was not under the vigilance of the House of Contracts of Seville, in charge of registering all traffic of the run to the Indies. Many left from the Canary Islands, particularly from the Island of Palms, taking along many slaves that usually remained in America.

There were complaints about the lack of justice administration and of His Majesty's orders: "Every day more Portuguese caravels arrive in Cape Verde laden with Negroes against that ordered and prohibited by Your Majesty, and because I said that the orders are not well complied with they want to stone me."[50]

"Among the Spanish authorities there were probably some who were in favor of legalizing this illegal situation, considering that promotion of

---

[48] Proodian García de, Lucía, *Los Judíos en América, sus Actividades en los virreinatos de Nueva Castilla y de Nueva Granada, siglo XVII,* Madrid, 1966.
[49] *Ibidem,* p. 28.
[50] Bataillon, Marcel, "Santo Domingo era Portugal", in *Historia y Sociedad en el Mundo de Habla Española,* homage to José Miranda, Bernardo García Martínez, *et al,* Editores, México, El Colegio de México, 1970, p. 116 (taken from A.G.I., R.I., page 308, Francisco de Vera to Don Jerónimo de Ulloa, from His Majesty's counsel and his attorney in the Royal Council of Indies. De la Palma, Aug. 17, 1565.

economic life demanded the presence of more settlers besides an always desirable increase in the number of Negro slaves."[51]

"Not even those who were arrested desisted of their intentions. Two procedures much in use to evade orders are known: the first consisted of immigrants who thanks to help from those already residing in the Indies managed to get married with 'women of the city', while in jail awaiting to be embarked, which made their residing in the neighborhood easier or at least of obtaining a license to remain in the city; the second was by gaining freedom under bail, forcing them not to leave the city, which they did not comply with, going into the interior of the country. Once escape was discovered, the bondsman paid the amount required, thereby ending the affair."[52]

Many Judaizers went to New Spain through Spanish ports, in the Canary Islands or through some Caribbean island. At the beginning they arrived from Spain, but the greater majority arrived from Portugal. Since 1580, date in which Portugal became part of the Spanish crown, a huge number of converts sailed to the Indies as Spanish citizens. Since 1529 Charles V had allowed ships to sail from Coruña, Bayona, Avilés, Laredo, Bilbao, San Sebastian and Malaga so as to promote immigration and commerce. Those conditions continued until 1573. But even after 1573 there were illicit exits from the northern ports.

Lea, the great historian, said referring to the ban of going to America: "The prohibitions for converted Jews, heretics, Moors or reconciled Jews to immigrate to the Indies were rigorous and continuous from the beginning of the discovery and conquest. They were prescribed to Commander Ovando in 1501, reiterated by the Solicitors of Hispaniola in 1508, insisting on them in 1518 and finally they were extended to the grandchildren of those who had been subjected to the Holy Office. And yet, even since 1509 a legal economic type of crack began opening, a type of composition that allowed new Christians to go to the New World and work their trade there."

---

[51] *Ibidem.*
[52] Proodian, *op. cit.,* p. 29.

"However, it was only after the second half of the 16th century that Philip II became really worried about the situation of New Spain. Travelers from everywhere began arriving there. An attempt at Jewish colonization alarmed New Spain's viceroy."[53]

Philip II took a stern attitude. He founded the tribunal of the Holy Office as a stable institution and charged its organization to a trustworthy officer to whom he conferred full powers whose name was Pedro Moya de Contreras.

Life in the Colony

The first Jewish inhabitants of the American Continent may be classified into three groups:

The first one comprises those converts that had accepted Christianity as a religion for the security of their success and lives (considering that it was not convenient to keep any ties with Judaism). This group included not only those indifferent to religious matters, but also those apostates that so much contributed to the misfortune of their previous brethren. It is very difficult to find their traces; they generally came from Spain.

The second nucleus was composed of Crypto-Jews or converts who had had the Christian religion imposed them on and who remained faithful to their old faith. These include the converts who came from Spain and Portugal. This group can be called that of "converts by imposition" and it also includes two subgroups: the "forbidden ones", that is, who descended from families with a history in the Inquisition and the second, that of Castilian Judaizers, "those who lacked such a history in the Holy Office and

---

[53] Medina, José Toribio, *Historia del Tribunal del Santo Oficio de la Inquisición en México,* 2nd ed. Expanded by Julio Jiménez Rueda. Mexico, Ediciones Fuente Cultural, 1952. p. 78.

so had no obstacle to enter, being free to use the privileges that had been granted them as subjects of the Castilian kingdom."[54]

The third group was made up of Jews and converts who had settled in the lands of Holland and England, or any place of the Ottoman Empire and who had commercial relations or contacts with the New World. Some of them spent terms of two or more years in the American dominions. After the expulsion from Spain when ships replete with the proscribed Jews sailed the seas, "A Marrano colony, composed of 37 families, existed in London around 1540, but it was denounced and dispersed in 1542."[55]

The feelings of nobility and distinction were common in the 15th century to both Christians and Jews and accompanied them in their exile.

To protect themselves against suspicion or persecution from old Christians, "new Christians" decisively promoted their consciousness of caste as a shield from their own Jewish descent, as justification against society and for their own sincerity in their Christianity. But "old Christians" were still angry when seeing that in spite of the expulsion and conversions, new Christians still continued occupying important positions.

Thus, in the 16th and 17th centuries "blood purity" became the backbone of noble and ecclesiastic society as a result of the issues introduced by converts.

We must recognize among converts various groups or sectors insofar as degree of intensity of faith. But, generally demands of feelings were imposed in some way, as could not but happen at a time where nothing stood before religion.

The convert belonged to a different group, distinct in habits from old Christians and even from Jews: "they obeyed those Judaic rites, which with great ignorance and danger in their souls, they kept neither one nor another

---

[54] Proodian, *op. cit.,* p. 42.

[55] Poliakov, Leon, *Historia del Antisemitismo, desde Cristo hasta los Judíos de la Corte,* Buenos Aires, Editorial Siglo Veinte, 1968, p. 215.

law; because they did not get circumcised as Jews, as is urged in the Old Testament and although they kept the Sabbath and fasted some fasts, and if they did some rite did not do another one, so in one or another law they lied. And if in some cases the husband failed some Jewish ceremony and the wife was a good Christian; a son or daughter were good Christians and another one Jewish. And within the home there was a variety of beliefs and one covered for the other."[56]

Converts lived in permanent dread; they desired to go back to their religion and constantly hoped for a miracle. Their lives were full of terror from fear of being discovered for still practicing some of the rites of their old faith and they were in awe of God for sinning against His law and being apparently Christian.

In the home of converts there was usually a son who was a friar, because having someone within the Christian clergy helped converts mask their situation; but this by itself created unpleasantness inside because they had to hide in their own home to celebrate any Jewish ceremony.

"…. And they were under the hope of the people of Israel when they were in Egypt; that although they had many humiliations, they hoped that God would bring them out from among them and because He later took them out with strong and extended arm; and so they believed that by God's hand they would be led, visited and taken out to the Holy Land of Promise, so these crazy hopes were and lived among Christians, as was stated and confessed by them in such a way that all the lineage remained defamed and touched by that disease."[57]

Since the expulsion, life for converts acquired a dual character; they were "new Christians" outdoors but continued being Jews at heart.

---

[56] Del Pulgar, Hernando, *Crónica de los Reyes Católicos,* Valencia (s.e.), 1870, p. 210; López Martínez, *op. cit.*, p. 151.

[57] Bernáldez, Andrés, *Historia de los Reyes Católicos, apud.* in López Martínez, *op. cit.*, p. 159.

Every so often edicts were read that all citizens had to listen to, which enumerated the uses, habits and practices of Judaizers, threatening the citizens with punishment and excommunication to those who did not denounce them to the Holy Office.

"We order you to denounce before Us if you know or have heard it said that some people keep Saturdays in observance of the Law of Moses, wearing those days clean or improved clothing, setting the table with a clean tablecloth and putting clean sheets on the bed in honor of Saturday, not lighting fires or anything else, keeping it since Friday evening. Or their having discarded the meat they were to eat. Or their having cut the throat of the beef or fowl they were to eat, first testing the knife with the nail to see if it is sharp. Or their having eaten meat during Lent and other days forbidden by the Church, without any need to do so. Or their having fasted during the great fast of Jews that they call of atonement, walking shoeless that day. Or that they pray Jewish prayers and at night ask for forgiveness from one another, the parents putting their hands on the children's heads to sanctify them. Or if they fast the fast of Queen Esther and other Jewish fasts in the middle of the week, such as Monday or Thursday, not eating meat and washing their hands the day before those fasts, cutting their nails and the tips of their hair, keeping them or burning them with Jewish prayers. Or if they bless the table according to Jewish rites. Or if saying some Hebrew words each one drinking a sip from one sole wine glass. Or if they prayed the Psalms of David without Gloria Patri. Or if they wait for the Messiah. Or if some woman keeps forty days after giving birth without entering the Temple. Of if when a baby is born, he is circumcised and given a Jewish name. Or if they wash, after being baptized, the place where the priest put the oil. Or if some are married the Jewish way. Or if when some person is about to die they turn his head towards the wall and when dead they wash him with hot water, shaving off his beard and underarms. Or if they throw water in the house of the dead. Or if they eat off the floor, behind doors, fish and olives and no meat. Or if someone has said that the Law of Moses is as good as that of Christ."[58]

Passions in that century of controversies and theological arguments were red hot and any detail, even a totally insignificant one, served to doubt about the author's orthodoxy, particularly if he was a new Christian.

Rodrigo Henríquez de Fonseca, already married, heard the following advice from his father: "The first thing you and your family must not do is communicate with those Portuguese merchants, rabbis, nor admit their visit nor that of their wives so they won't discover the Law you keep or you will be lost if you do not keep it very secret within your heart; second, don't slight the God of Christians, their saints and ceremonies, because everyone feels the slight of his God and His Law, and don't venture being discovered because then you will not be servicing God; third, do not make a ceremony of the Law of Moses, because it is done imperfectly and then it is not in God's service, just as keeping the Sabbath; and God who took away the Law from the Jews because of their idolatry and atrociousness, He does not want it kept imperfectly until He wills its return, recognizing that the captivity we suffer is just because of our sins and only the humble heart serves and performing the ceremonies only serves to venture and be discovered."[59]

The fear of being discovered was often stronger than their desire to keep the Sabbath or fast in some holiday. They were conscious that they were unable to perform the ceremonies with the precision required by the Law and that these had many imperfections; they were aware that it was divine punishment and that God would soon redeem their suffering.

---

[58] Lewin, Boleslao, *La Inquisición en México, siglos XVI y XVII,* 2 Vols. Buenos aires, Editorial Cajics, 1967, pp. 43-44.

[59] Process against Rodrigo Henríquez de Fonseca to Don Diego Sotelo, accused as Judaizer, processed on August 30, 1656. Sentence, Public Auto-da-Fe, 1664, reconciled. Tribunal of the Kings in A.H.N., Inquisition, book 1031, page 398-414; *apud.* in Proodian, *op. cit.* p. 181.

Portuguese converts were more able to keep Jewish rites because they were granted twenty years of grace and renewed once more. When one discovered another convert both recommended absolute secrecy. Keeping silent was for everyone's sake because their own saying was "Judaizers are like cherries, when you pull one all the others come down in a string." Daily life was very peculiar due to the constant fear to which they were subjected. They never kept letters or papers at home so as not to have anything to compromise them. They had no prayer books or Bibles and if they did, they hid them in the darkest holes. Business owners often had to work or open on Saturdays to avoid suspicion. They also had to pretend while eating; whenever they ate bacon before their non-Jewish neighbors or friends they would come home and vomit.

Preparing for the Sabbath included cutting the nails from hands and feet; these clippings were burned. It was a must to use clean sheets and shirts on that day. That habit was holy. In spite of the impossibility of fully complying with religious observance, converts respected Jewish Law and tried to keep it as well as possible.

Family gatherings were important to preserve certain festivities; the women would prepare the food according to dietetic laws and they tried to give the day off to the servants.

Family ties were strengthened when they gathered to eat, particularly when having some large festivity. Community gatherings were an intrinsic element in the life of new Christians. Fasting together provided them with some diversion because it was not quite the same as fasting by oneself.

Three practices were very common: purchasing new dishes for the festivity of Passover, because Jews are forbidden to use the same dishes that are used the rest of the year; by accidentally breaking those dishes that were earthenware, little by little, they had a good pretext to buy another set. Another habit was that of buying new clothes before the Jewish New Year; these clothes were used particularly on the Day of Atonement or the Great Fast, considered the most sacred of all days.

In this stealthy life of subterfuge, converts lived during the centuries that followed their expulsion from the Motherland. They tried to keep their Judaism despite numberless sacrifices. At the beginning, they hid from their children their real faith. But as the date of the boys' thirteenth birthday (*Bar Mitzvah)* approached and the boy would begin to form part of Jewish Law as an adult, he had to be told about his true religion. There were very few inquisitorial cases that talked about this habit among converts, because performing it was a real danger both for the boy as well as the whole family. One or two years beforehand he was taught everything concerning the Law, his obligations as a Jew before God and his people. If he had not been circumcised, they tried to do so before he became thirteen or during the next year.

Dr. Proodian mentions: "….. we felt amazed and even admiring of the immense vitality of these people that in such adverse circumstances, so inappropriate for their purposes, not only did they not submit and remain passive, but on the contrary, they went on the offensive trying to gain new associates into their lines. Doubtlessly, their proselytizing constituted a powerful underground current that undermined the heterogeneous and boisterous colonial society."[60]

Although their lives as Jews always remained absolutely secret, a convert always knew about others. Even those arriving from distant lands could always find food and lodging in a short time. They helped each other at the time when the Inquisition had still not been officially installed in the New World; Francisco Millán had a tavern and all the converts of New Spain would visit him, drink some wine, chat for a while or borrow some money.

It is easy to understand the life of these people and their faithfulness to Judaism in a time of great religiosity. People were normal if they were religious; if they were heretic, they were abnormal. The axis of resistance of marranos to fully convert to Christianity was their belief that the Messiah had

---

[60] Proodian, *op. cit.,* p. 188.

still not arrived…. If the Messiah had really arrived all their suffering would have been in vain.

Converts exerted a great influence over Spanish mentality. Perhaps this influence and the victory over the Moors gave the Spaniards the same characteristic of a Messianic people, the chosen people.

America appeared as the prize for Christian faith.

However, for the Jews, their suffering, among others in the world, was the best demonstration that the Messiah had not yet arrived in "this vale of tears." For the Spaniard, the messianic attitude was reflected in his feeling as redeemer of men in the new lands.

The obsession of converts became polarized around the vague ideas and deep feelings about their salvation through the Law and, particularly, about their messianism. Jewish and Christian religious practices became utterly mixed up.

At the beginning it was their habit to cover their head but pretty soon it fell into disuse. Preliminary ablutions through which Judaism made cleanliness precede its relationship with the divinity continued being used and for a long time was taken as proof that whoever practiced it was a Judaizer. Turning towards the East and covering the head with a white sheet to pray, similar to the traditional stole or *Talit,* were practices that survived until a very advanced time; however, kneeling during the service, contrary to Jewish practice, prevailed in such a way that it received special mention in the liturgy. Prayers were recited rather than sung, the ancient chants were probably forgotten so as not to call attention to the singers.

Converts insisted on the eternal existence of one sole merciful God who promulgated the Decalogue on Mount Sinai; if He did not change, the Law could not be transformed either.

Judaizers complied with a series of religious rites and practices that embraced both religions: the Jewish and the Christian, although the spirit that encouraged them by practicing both was very different. It was difficult to perform these ceremonies.

For Sabbath prayers or those of any other festivity the presence of ten men was necessary. This is called a *Minyan* (ten is the number existing in God). They had no need of a synagogue as long as they could have a Bible to read and ten men were together. This was usually done in some house hiding away from the eyes of servants.

Ceasing all work was exceedingly difficult for these converts. Of course, those who could not avoid it did not work on Saturday going to their house of business only as a feint.

Keeping the Sabbath meant abstaining from work, which was a real danger for any man, because not opening his shop was a distinct clue of his being a Judaizer.

Women tried to cook and do their domestic errands on Friday so as not to do them the next day. There is a dish known by the name of Adafina[61] that is prepared on Friday and kept in the oven until Saturday. Some women were so religious that they even cut the bread on Friday so as not to do so on Saturday.

Food was very different from that of old Christians because converts refrained from eating certain foods considered impure by the Law of Moses. They would not eat those ruminating animals whose hoof is not cloven such as rabbits and others; but they would eat animals that did have it like beef or mutton, etc. Meat had to have the fat removed and be drained of blood, set in water for an hour and after draining it had to be salted for an hour. If meat were not prepared this way, it could not be eaten.

They also abstained from eating of those animals that have a nerve or a small body in glandular tissue next to the liver. Animals had to be

---

[61] Adafina or Hamia was made with fat meat, chickpeas, lima beans, green beans, hard bones and any other legume.

slaughtered using a knife exclusively for that purpose and they were positioned facing the East. Jews were forbidden to eat swine flesh.

Converts were very careful to refrain from eating meat if the animal had not been ritually slaughtered by a Jewish butcher with a keen knife without dents "….separating the meat into filaments and taking off the sciatic nerve."

From generation to generation, converts took care of a number of rites: to set in the threshold of their homes certain signs (*Mezuzah,* this was very rarely found in New Spain) or to get married the Judaic way before performing the Catholic ceremony. Funeral rites were particularly watched and so, riskier.

a) *Taharah* (washing the body and wrapping it in a white shroud).

b) When somebody died, the close family would rip its clothes as a sign of mourning, keeping ritual duel during seven days and eating only fish and eggs.

c) Spraying water in the house of the dead. In the coffin, the head had to lie on a pillow of earth that they tried to get from the "Holy Land."[62]

They tried to keep the feasts to coincide with the Hebrew calendar but it was often difficult because they had none at hand. Among these there was:

Kippur, also called the Great Day of Forgiveness or Atonement, is the greatest Jewish festivity. This date had to be ten days after the September moon. In reality it is a day of meditation and atonement. A very rigorous fast was made from the setting of the sun until the first star appeared on the morrow. It is the most sacred day in Jewish religion.

Besides this fast there were many others "….they fast the fast of Queen Esther, whom they call the Loss of the Holy Thing and other fasts in the middle of the week, such as Mondays and Thursdays, not eating those days

---

[62] Liebman, Seymour, *Los Judíos y América Central (Fe Llamas e Inquisición),* Buenos Aires, Siglo Veintiuno Editores, 1971, p. 442.

until the evening when the star comes out and those nights not eating meat, and a day earlier, they wash for the fast, cutting their nails and the tips of their hair and they pray Jewish prayers moving the head up and down, turning towards the wall and before praying they wash their hands in water.... and they dress in twill, serge or linen with certain strings hanging."[63]

Judaizers living in the Indies used to fast twice a week (*Taanit Beab)* doing it even when they were somewhere on a trip or when incarcerated in the Inquisitorial jail. This was usually done as an offering to the Lord so that some desire would occur.

Fasts seem to come from way back in antique times, because there are traces of this practice in Zechariah and they were used when a great calamity befell the people of Israel.

Other festivities were celebrated such as the Passover Lamb, when they recalled the Jews in their captivity in Egypt and their exit thanks to the strong arm of God. The *Haggadah* or the *Book of Esther* had to be read which was difficult to keep around in America without arousing suspicions.

For New Spanish Jews, the obstacles that hindered practice of their faith openly felt like spiritual slavery.

Jews in the New World tried to follow all the habits, they literally expected that God would free them just as he had done to the Jews in Egypt and would send the redeemer. They ate unleavened bread known as *Matzah* (plural Matzoth) that reminded Jews of the bread their brethren had eaten in the desert after leaving Egypt. A number of physicians prescribed this "lean bread" to stomach patients, so on the week when it had to be eaten, they pretended to be sick without requiring any explanation.

---

[63] López Martínez, Nicolás, *Los Judaizantes Castellanos y la Inquisición en Tiempos de Isabel la Católica,*
Burgos, 1954, p. 180.

Jewish religion has always formed part of individual lives; at birth boys had to be circumcised. But circumcision in the New World was not done when babies were eight days old, it was sometimes done anywhere from age eight to fourteen.

They also tried to have a wedding done in a Jewish ceremony. To marry they tried especially hard to find people of the same religion so they could later continue practicing Judaism without problems.

Other rites included the habit of washing hands before meals and as a Mosaic practice they kept it rigorously. They also washed their hands and faces before saying the morning prayers and they covered their heads while praying.

There were few Bibles circulating at the time in New Spain. Some people had access to translations such as the *Vulgate* which was more frequent.

The processes show various prayers recited by converts, particularly one known as *Amidah* that in Hebrew means to be standing. The weekly prayer is known as the "18 blessings". This must be said while standing with the feet together. So, in the process of Pedro Arias de Maldonado, he was accused of having stood with some boards between his feet so that he could not move them while praying.[64]

One of the prayers appearing more often in the processes is the one that reads: "Hear, Oh Israel, the Lord our God, the Lord is One."

The prayer of *Shmah* fervently repeated every morning and in the evening prayers and recited by every observer as the last conscious act of his life symbolizes a life dedicated to honoring God: "Hear, Oh, Israel, the Lord our God, the Lord is One." With this prayer we testify that God is one and only. This prayer also reminds Jews that God is a spiritual being. According to this prayer, if God is one and man is one, men can only be ruled by an ethical

---

[64] Liebman, Seymour, "*Sephardic ethnicity in the Spanish New World colonies*" in the *Congreso de Americanistas,* September, 1974, p. 10.

principle, that is, ethics will rule over all men in the earth under all circumstances.

Jews who pronounce this prayer aspire to something further than the mundane; through this prayer they have achieved putting together the deepest in Jewish religious belief.

Constant association with Catholic practices produced a mixture of rites among Judaizers. New habits developed that were influenced by their external adherence to Christianity.

Apocrypha was held in the same level as the Old Testament. Reciting some Biblical passages became a way of praying. Sometimes, prayers from Catholic liturgy were borrowed to be used in Judaism. A person who would go by a prayer meeting would have thought that they were all Christians praying because even the music had been adapted.

Social integration of this group of Jewish converts into colonial society in the process of formation was relatively easy because they could pass just like any other white European or Spaniard. They had certain prerogatives that were easy to acquire by their looks alone.

Once they managed to occupy some important position the situation changed radically because they would appear as new Christians, converts or Crypto-Jews. New Christians were decidedly scorned by New Spanish society, even more than in previous centuries, which did not make their integration any easier. This state of affairs became worse and worse impinging contact amid huge differences, revaluing hierarchical positions to the maximum degree which drove people mostly from the middle of the 16th century and throughout the 17th to conquer the highest level of social consideration whereby they sought to demonstrate blood purity particularly in high offices and in every kind of popular guilds and fraternities.

These points of view and the traditional bias, with hermetic closure for anything that did not fit those principles sustained by the greater part of Spanish society, created around new Christians a dense atmosphere that oppressed them, making them feel "ideologically and practically displaced from the environment in which they lived and in a position of inferiority before the other citizens of the colony...."[65]

The stigma of "new Christian" was always present. The supposed integration that would occur when they converted never became true. Even in the New World, converts continued being different, appearing as a problem for the Crown and the viceroys. As long as they could hide their identity, there was no problem and yet many opportunities that as peninsular Spaniards or Creoles they could get, but they were always on the alert, fearful of being discovered and shunned from society because of their beliefs and habits.

In their character as foreigners and practicing a different religious creed, converts were banned from access to public positions. As foreigners ".... they could not colonize lands nor settle in towns; no commercial relations could be made with them, either by themselves or through an agent; even those who by special license had been able to cross the previous prohibitions could not obtain Indians, receive privileges or ecclesiastical benefits.

In spite of these very severe prohibitions, from the very beginning they were able to go to the Indies with the first conquerors, to receive Indians in grants (such as Cortes granted Hernando Alonso for his participation in the conquest); to enter the clergy and to occupy relevant positions, sometimes even the most prominent ones in New Spain inside the religious orders themselves.

All this required a very difficult balancing act over the Law's trapeze, getting false information from old Christians, changing the place of birth on paper so as to obstruct pertinent inquiries and avert possible suspicions.

At the time, it was an authorized habit to purchase public positions that had no jurisdiction, which presented an opportunity to integrate into Mexican society. This position meant marriages among the most prominent Creoles

---

[65] Proodian, *op. cit.,* pp. 128-129.

and the occasion to buy land and assets, which would allow them to form part of colonial society.

Status within society was determined by economic activities in which each person was involved. To present a counterweight to the disadvantage of being a new Christian, converts made every possible effort to obtain positions and to establish relations with people of good economic situations.

Through these marriages they managed to consolidate their position within colonial society, seeking women of important family lines, because their culture and station made it easy for those young men to be accepted.

If the convert practiced the Law of Moses, he considered that the union would be transitory because in due time he would wed someone who professed his Law. Besides, within his tradition, those marriages were null because they would never be accepted by any rabbi or confirmed unless the spouse were ready to accept that Law.

Wives who had some suspicion about their husbands' ideas ceased viewing them as the beloved, transforming them into despicable beings with whom living was undesirable and who carried along the loss of reputation and social position.

Education and culture

A typical characteristic of Jews was to provide their children the most painstaking education. "He who does not teach his son a profession is as if he taught him to steal", says the Talmud.

New Christians greatly endeavored to give their children a good education that would provide them with the principles that had been lacking in their lives and that, in spite of their good economic position, they sometimes missed. This educational task began in infancy, so the generations born in the New World always had teachers available in charge of their learning. When lacking teachers their mother would instruct them or send them to schools for

Creoles and their children where they were very well prepared and from where they would be able to study in university classrooms. There are many cases in the files of young men at the university who professed the Law of Moses and were accused of Judaizing.

Those who did not desire going the long way of university life usually continued the merchant profession of their fathers.

As has already been mentioned, there was always the issue of sending one of the children to a religious order, so this was seen as an element to distract attention from the inquisitors. This child had usually no knowledge of the parents' religious ideas.

Education was of two kinds: lay, where all the subjects taught belonged to the human knowledge of the time and religious, begun when they attained their majority. In men it occurred at thirteen and in women at twelve; education provided at home at a time when servants would not be aware of it. They taught the youngsters how to keep the rites and traditions of the Law of Moses, the dietary laws, habits for marriage, for circumcision and for death, traditions transmitted from generation to generation.

During the first centuries of Spanish dominion in America, almost all the converts practicing the Law of Moses learned the Psalms and the verses recited in various occasions by heart. Very few of them had any sacred books or even knew of them, so learning was carried on by oral tradition.

In the 17th century a new type of heresy appeared: enlightenment ideas began penetrating into the American colonies. Veiled matters and those reserved for lettered men of irreproachable faith and clergy of recognized orthodoxy started being talked about by spirits more accessible to their doubts burning inside. Boats arrived with books that were read with eagerness; the books of astrology and occult arts in general reveal the small heterodox, fearful people subject to astrological dreams.

The Inquisition granted permits to read forbidden works to certain people. We know that in the 17th century editions of the Holy Writ unauthorized by the Church were circulating although they were set in the index of forbidden books. This allows us to understand the spirit that animated converts at the end of the 17th century and the beginning of the 18th.

Just like the Spaniards of that time, converts had a great interest in knowing everything that referred to the new science that was appearing in Europe and that was rapidly being propagated in America, besides the Holy Writings.

The Inquisition became very worried about processing all those who were reading the prohibited works and this did not mean only Judaizers. At that moment, knowledge and faith found themselves facing a common enemy, so the struggles of both had similar facets.

According to Seymour Liebman, there were five basic principles that permitted Jewish survival in American soil:

1. Their adherence to messianism and their religious beliefs.
2. Their belief in the Biblical Mandates and the denomination as "chosen people".
3. The existence of endogamy and the role performed by Jewish women.
4. The "farda" (a special tax on Jews and Moors) and its contribution to revive culture.
5. Spiritual oppression and its effects over Jewish Spanish people.[66]

Judaizers were always hoping for the arrival of the Messiah. They never accepted the fact that Jesus Christ had been the Messiah because their idea about the Redeemer constantly mentioned that at His arrival peace would reign on earth for everybody, but for the Jew, suffering continued.

---

[66] Liebman, *op. cit.*, p. 10.

Women in colonial life

The role of Jewish women in the development of colonial life in keeping the traditions and religion was of vital importance. Many women were barely thirteen or fourteen years old when they married. When there were no rabbis in New Spain, the couple solemnized their wedding through a contract written in the presence of family and friends. This contract was made according to Jewish law and later on, when they found a rabbi, he repeated the wedding ceremony and added certain blessings for the couple.

It was easier for her to observe certain rites and habits than for her husband because he was always afraid of being discovered more easily in his job.

Chicken slaughter was done according to Jewish Law. The women frequently were the ones to kill the fowl.

The habit of removing the fat from meat led many Jewish women to be discovered as heretics.

"Elena de Silva, also known as Elena López, was a pious woman that made *Matzoth* for Passover". Before Passover of 1641, she and her daughter Isabel were surprised by a Catholic neighbor while preparing unleavened bread". This Elena de Silva observed the Jewish Law of visiting at funerals and providing food for the mourners during the period of mourning.[67]

Women usually washed the bodies of dead women and sometimes also of men according to the Jewish ritual. "During some time, during the 17th century, one or two women acted to shroud men. This can be understood because fear of being discovered became so acute that it became an obsession after 1642.

Besides shrouding the body of the deceased, women usually had the task of sewing the shrouds for the members of their family. "In first place, the cloth had to come from either Holland or Rouen, France, where there were

---

[67] Liebman, *Los Judíos...,* pp. 94-95.

Jewish textile manufactures who could guarantee they were not violating the Law of *Shatnes*, the Biblical ban on mixing two types of material for Jewish attire."[68]

Woman was the guiding star of the home, the one responsible for transmitting the love of religion and devotion to children so Judaism would not be lost in the New World.

Frequently it was only a woman who was capable of haranguing the fainthearted men who were sick and tired of struggling. There was some inner force of spiritual values in those women who were able to instill their values in the children, America's Creoles. "And all that without programs, without their ever having had anybody to educate them, who could lead them into that untried life, because everything was new, unforeseen, distant, excessive. "….She became used to all types of risks, to tragic news, to loneliness, to widowhood."[69]

The farda

The farda is defined in old Spanish dictionaries as a form of tribute or tax paid by Jews and Moslems to maintain their respective communities in the Holy Land.

In the process of three men of New Spain (Ruy Díaz Nieto, Diego Díaz Nieto and Tomás Treviño de Sobremonte) there are references to the farda but, in reality, it is difficult to understand how it was done in the New World.

We suppose that there were emissaries who arrived in New Spain from the Holy Land. They were usually sages of great culture who remained somewhere for a length time, enough to study with the inhabitants; and after concluding their stay they collected money to maintain the Jewish

---

[68] Liebman, *Valerosas Cripto-Judías en la América Colonial,* Buenos Aires, Biblioteca Popular Judía, núm. 66, 1973, p. 32.

[69] Borges, Ana Lola, *"La Mujer Pobladora en los Orígenes Americanos",* in *Anuario de Estudios Americanos,* Sevilla, 1972, Separata del T. XXIX, p. 429.

communities in the Holy Land. This tradition helped strengthen Judaism by instilling fresh knowledge into the people and kept up their identity with the Promised Land.

The discovery of America gave the Spaniards access to a huge territory from which they imported enormous amounts of precious metals and from which they obtained important commercial advantages.

Spanish merchants were limited to being intermediaries who bought wares abroad to resell them in the provinces dominated by the tip of the Spanish Empire.

In 1522, mining began in New Spain so the Spaniards devoted themselves almost exclusively to exploiting precious metals from these mines.

Spain claimed, uselessly, for its empire to produce only for its sole benefit. Thus, it forbade raising a number of agricultural products and all manufacturing and it established a commercial monopoly in all its territories.

A good part of the wealth extracted in America was removed from circulation with the result that it increased the power and influence of the aristocracy and the clergy.

The economic regime introduced by the Spaniards into the Colony was characterized by a number of things: work in the mines which was the basic economic activity that reached its highest development during three centuries; in agriculture and cattle raising, extensive exploitation reigned, employing a very large amount of land; the Colony raised enough produce for its own consumption most of which went to the Spanish and European landed gentry and the people of mixed race to supply the cities.

Commerce

Free and direct contracting between the ports of the Indies and foreign markets able to supply them was forbidden. Spain determined that only it and, in some cases, those merchants who had signed a trade treaty could devote themselves to providing products for the colonies, at the same time reciprocating with gold and silver to compensate for the supplies provided.

This exchange was regulated by the Contracting House of Seville and to control this commerce more efficiently, articles were not to be transported from one site to another arbitrarily but rather in fleet convoys.

A certain type of merchant began emerging through whose hands passed all the products to be had in the Indies. Converts figured very highly in this group of merchants who had arrived in the New World.

During the first few years they lacked assets and any lucrative employment, the only thing they owned was a "shoulder cape" and often enough not even that because they were frequently in "bankruptcy from debts". Their habitual trade was as hawker, that meant to "go about peddling a witches' brew of things in the street" or cheap merchandise; normally they were a spectacle to see them ambling miserably through the populous and well-marked streets with their sales bag hanging from the shoulder. Most of them suffered greatly from hunger, perhaps dying in some unknown place in that vast territory.

Immigrants of the next generation began to raise their living standard progressively, laboriously working without rest while facing all the obstacles that appeared before them. From hawkers they went to owning a stand or shed, later on a shop and by 1625 their influence began to be felt in the viceroyalty's commerce.

One thing characterized them all: their solidarity, "help your brother in disgrace". Beginning with whoever made a small discount at the shop to the powerful merchant residing in the Netherlands who offered a loan to a Spanish merchant for some enterprise; "including the merchant that from Mexico sent his wares to Peru in the name of a Lima trader, selected among others because he had a wife and daughter in San Juan de Luz, sure to be a member of 'The Carda' which in their argot meant anybody who Judaized..."[70]

Although they arrived disoriented without having any idea about investing their scarce coins, they guardedly found out about some contact with their brethren and, upon finding them, they knew they would be available to protect and guide their first steps in America.

There were close relations among American converts with those of Holland, England and the countries of the Ottoman Empire, Spain and Portugal. Among all these, they performed great commercial transactions of every type; in the 17th century boats of New Spanish converts sailed over the oceans towards European countries looking for merchandise to buy and sell.

Assets of converts were usually movable or portable. Since their life was a constant speedy "displacement" from one location to another leaving everything behind, it made them develop the possibility of accumulating assets that could be rapidly taken so that upon arriving elsewhere they would have something to fall back on and could easily begin all over again. Their commercial success caused the admiration of their fellow citizens. They faced the dangers of the road, the lack of safety, the imperfect means of transport of the times and the weather differences existing between one place and another with equanimity.

When they were being persecuted by the officers of the Holy Office, they would usually move immediately to another city, that is, if they resided in New Spain, a few years later they could be found in Peru or vice versa.

One of the main sources of income in the New World for converts was selling clothing that could be of various kinds: "from the damask of Castile or China, to some narrow lace edging or multicolored passementerie, including between the two ends some coarse cotton cloth, taffeta pieces,

---

[70] Proodian, *op. cit.,* p. 69.

knitted stockings, musk, Castilian clothes and knits and clothing material..."[71]

Occasionally it was not the owner of the clothes shop who sold directly, but he would give it over to someone else on credit so the latter could begin working and get some income. There was no material, article or anything else that could not be used for selling by converts, who accomplished these transactions with great commercial ability.

These people performed an important role in the economic development of New Spain since the middle of the 16th century. Robert Ricard writes in his work that "they were the main merchants, both wholesale and retail; they implemented the traffic between Mexico and the mining centers such as Sultepec (east of Mexico), Pachuca, Taxco, Tlalpujahua (east of Michoacán) and Zacatecas. A passage in a process specifies that Sebastián Rodríguez had commercial ties between New Spain and China. It is remarkable that there were two physicians, Manuel and Antonio Morales, uncle and nephew, and various artisans, three silver workers, two soap manufacturers, two tailors, a manufacturer of string articles and one making knives..."[72]

During the last years of the 16th century, slave traffic with the New World grew to a very great extent. This commerce was made under the Crown's control and it was considered a perfectly legal trade just like any other.

Imports were made by means of a contract signed by the Spanish Crown and a merchant who agreed to transport to America, during a fixed time, a certain number of Negroes.

There were many new Christians who obtained licenses to devote themselves to the transport and sale of Negroes; the second phase of the slave trade began when the vessel landed and the royal office factor visited the ship

---

[71] *Ibidem,* p. 76.
[72] Ricard, Robert, *Pour un Étude de Judaïsme Portugais au Mexique pendant le Période Coloniale",* p. 524, *apud.* in Liebman, *Los Judíos en...,* p. 181.

and once having complied with all due formalities approved for the cargo of Negroes to be sold in the markets located in the various New Spanish cities.

When the sellers were foreigners, generally Portuguese, they were prohibited from going inland, ban which they usually disregarded.

For Jewish converts this occupation became an escape route to rid themselves of the Inquisition, because they remained in the Indies only long enough to finish selling their wares and went back to the sea. This way it was difficult to track them.

Converts were engaged in the slave trade as agents on both Iberian kingdoms because they had the facility of being able to bring slaves from the Portuguese areas in Africa and usually to sell them directly in America without going through Spanish ports.

There are reasons to believe that the Catholic Monarchs knew that the converts were performing this trade that benefited the Crown and also that they acted as brokers for buying and selling slaves throughout New Spain.

Besides these commercial activities, converts traded in everything with everything: "corn, chocolate, sugar, flour, herbs, tobacco, prickly oxeye, tar, indigo, pearls, etc. and they also had contracts in silver mines, groceries and wine shops."[73] The latter item must have provided good earnings because many of them went into that business.

Mining had great influence in population distribution. Very soon the Crown's protective policies developed besides the fact that the territory was more abundantly supplied with silver than with gold mines. In the latter there had been no intervention of ecclesiastic credit, so this made it easier for Judaizers to go into the business.

In 1532 the mining districts of Taxco, Zacualpan, Zumpango del Río, Espíritu Santo and Tlalpujahua began operating. By the middle of the 16th century the second great mining districts constituted by Real del Monte in

---

[73] Proodian, *op. cit.*, p. 77.

Pachuca and Atotonilco were being actively exploited. The third one in Zacatecas began being mined in 1547 and in Guanajuato in 1554.

The most important population groups always grew around the mines, since they could congregate under the screen of mining exploitation. According to the processes studied in the Archivo General de la Nación, a great part of the population of those mining cities was of Jewish origin or they were Judaizers.

Mining guilds were highly favored by the legal regulations of the Spanish government. Miners enjoyed huge privileges. If a miner was apprehended he could not be removed from the place where the mineral was being exploited.

One or more Judaizers appeared in every trade existing within colonial society: Francisco Millán, at the beginning of the 16th century as tavern keeper; Juan Ríos inhabitant of Mexico performing the same work in 1601; Diego Flores as agent of the town of Xuchipila in 1594; Diego de Ocaña as clerk in 1578; tailors such as Daniel Benítez and Antonio Machado, Portuguese tailor by trade, originally from the city of Lisbon, living in Mexico City who was accused of Judaizing in 1601; José de Torres performing the task of soldier in Acapulco; Juan Rodríguez, a soap maker, was found in 1596 accused as Judaizer. Luis Díaz, silver craftsman, accused of Judaizing in 1597 and Jorge Díaz and Cristóbal Miguel, the latter separator of gold and silver.

The medical profession was almost totally monopolized by Jews and converts from the peninsula. When arriving in New Spain there are not so many appearing in that profession perhaps because it served as a clue to the Holy Office for their capture and yet we find several: Pedro Tinoco, physician accused in 1642; Manuel Morales, as Judaizer, accused by the Holy Office when the Carvajal family was accused.

There was one case of a Judaizer who sang in musical comedies. He was an inhabitant of Mexico City and he was accused of heresy in 1601. His name was Antonio López.

Juan Antonio Doria was coin minter in the Mint House until he was denounced to the Holy Office in 1601. Antonio Gómez, innkeeper in Mexico City, was accused in 1605.

Women also performed various trades: bakers, sewing women or gamblers. Margarita de Ribera had the trade of Infantry Guard and millstone maker. Margarita de Morera, inhabitant of Mexico City, working as mailwoman, was accused before the Holy Office in 1646.

Tomás Núñez de Peralta was son of Paxcual de Morera who was a tanner by trade.

To continue keeping Jewish traditions, there were converts in New Spain that worked as butchers and thus they appear in the processes of Simón Báez Sevilla who intervened in meat questions; Pedro Espinos, stagecoach and butcher in Mexico City who dealt in administering the butcher shops of Sayula.

Francisco López Blandón worked in gilding in Mexico City; he was processed in 1949. Gonzalo de León was a silver craftsman.

In most convert families there usually was some member dedicated to Christian religious matters. Many of them continued with their Judaizing practices and were processed.

Among the numerous processes existing in the Archivo General de la Nación, there is one of Simón Baez Bueno, ecclesiastic notary in the Puebla episcopate, on suspicion of being an enemy of the Holy Catholic Faith and another one of Luis Gómez, for having pretended being commissary of the Holy Office.

Life of converts in New Spain, contrary to that of followers of another religion, was similar to that of any European, with the advantage that they were determined to work at whatever there was, not just desiring honor and wealth; their integration took place at their time of arrival in the New World.

Cities with higher concentration of converts

Ethnic groups tend to get together in certain specific places when they are a minority.

The group of converts tried to congregate in the same city and within it in certain streets and quarters. Although at the beginning they arrived in the capital, they speedily tried to intern themselves within the Mexican territory, believing that this way they would be further away from the inquisitors.

There was almost no place of residence of Christian Spaniards where Judaizing families did not live as well. In the mining cities of Pachuca, Taxco, Zacatecas, Tlalpujahua, Sultepeque or Zultepec, Guanajuato and others, the processed were: Juan Pérez Quintana, constable major of the Temascaltepec mines; Juan de Figueroa, Portuguese in the Taxco mines; Fernando de Riva, constable major of the Taxco mines; Nicolás de Castro, Portuguese miner in the Zultepec mines, etc.

Residents of Mexico City had constant contact with miners of their same creed. The Carvajal family was one of the families that lived in Taxco for some time.

The nature itself of converts influenced them to try to live in border towns or ports, where it would be much easier to embark at any moment and they could develop any sort of trade. There was a large concentration in the port of Veracruz where we find Francisco Rodríguez Platero, also known as Rodríguez de Cea, the Texoso family, etc. These people helped the newcomers to New Spain providing them with information and asylum while they found some place to establish themselves.

There were other converts in Campeche and Yucatán through which they slipped in secret without having to present their "blood purity" credentials. There we find Juan González de Nogueira, Pedro Salinas and Fulana García who were processed as Judaizers.

In the neighborhood of Puebla de los Ángeles, there were large colonies of converts who had an intensive commerce with European countries such as Diego Núñez de Alvarado; Juan Adame, Portuguese accused of teaching an Indian how to take off the vein off a leg of mutton; Antonio Fernández, stonecutter.

There was a colony in Tlaxcala as shown in the process of Jerónimo Farfán who worked as painter and who lived in that city.

Among the one hundred Spanish families that Luis de Carvajal y de la Cueva brought to settle the northern part of the country; most were of convert origin. Many of those Sephardim settled in the lands of Nuevo León and Coahuila and a high percentage of the present-day population of that area descends from these converts. All these settlers of Sephardic origin were united by marriage between close relatives; a very reserved community of aristocratic character to which most public officers, military chiefs, agents and merchants belonged and which were the people of greater social significance.

A colony of Judaizer converts developed in the city of Guadalajara as well. There were Lorenzo de Machado, Francisco Navarro and many others.

Michoacán had Alonso Gómez living there; in Toluca, Francisco Tijera; in Oaxaca there was a large number of new Christians among whom the most prominent were Tomás Treviño de Sobremonte, Jerónimo Martín, Baltazar Hernández and many others.

Cities like Querétaro, León, etc. registered processes of people who celebrated Judaic rites. In León, Fray Diego Carrillo was accused of suspicion of being Jewish.

Acapulco was a port with a great amount of commercial movement because the ships that traded with the Philippines sailed from there. This port had a community of converts that was not very large, but it included some fervent Jews. It is difficult to calculate the size of the community since some of them spent only periods of time on land before embarking once again.

There was no place, no matter how small, where a new Christian could not be found, excepting of course those villages which were inhabited strictly by Indians.

Fray Tomás de Torquemada
First general inquisitor of Spain

Don Diego de Espinosa, Cardenal Bishop of Sigüenza
General inquisitor of Spain, year 1570

*El docto don Pedro Moya de Contreras, primer Inquisidor de Nueva España
y Arzobispo de México*

Auto General de la Fe en México (1649)

CHAPTER IV
IDEALISM AND PERSEVERANCE

Idealism and perseverance

Jews found pleasure in their religion; forced to make virtue of necessity, they found it a joyous activity. "The fact that they could distillate peace from pain and extract sweetness from bitterness was due to the intensity of their inner life."[74] Through the Law of Moses they had become the only heirs of absolute truth. And so, they had to serve as faithful guardians of the Law until the day would come when all humanity would obey it. To desert the Jewish people and abandon the Law was to commit treason against God.

At the end of days, when history would have concluded, when the sins of Israel had been atoned, the real Judge of nations would emit His final verdict. On that day, God would send the Messiah, son of David, and Israel would be restored to its ancient land in peace and security.

The hope for a final vindication has an incalculable power to encourage persistence. That is what breeds courage in martyrs. Converts found patience in their faith and so they hoped to be repaid with personal immortality. In times of crisis, when their cup overflowed with suffering, when it seemed that Israel could tolerate no more, in those moments their anxiety and Messianic hopes came to the fore. When their wish for liberation came close to a point of rupture, it procreated new feelings and a false Messiah appeared.

---

[74] Steimberg, Milton, *La Formación del Judío Moderno,* Mexico, 1963, p. 73.

The path of the Law helped make life easier thorough a system of habits and ceremonies: fast days and feast days followed one another in swift succession.

Happiness and grief of each individual were shared by everybody. Respect for life, consciousness of the rights of others, purity of family life, high standards of decency and honor, everything was explicitly described in the "Book", in the Law and the customs, where they learned that all moral greatness, all devotion to an "Ideal" was irretrievably linked to pain. This idea created a vivid impression in the minds of Jews of the time. They suffered because suffering was required for salvation. The theory of being chosen and of having a mission on earth invested them with a sensation of dignity and importance. Every aspect of life of the Jewish community reflected a climate of austerity and penitence.

The cult of martyrs, what was called the *Akedah,* constitutes one of the basic subjects of literature and for a long time it was the only theme of Jewish religious drama.

The cult of suffering, its systematic and reasoned value, its location at the level of divine punishment, but at the same time the expression of love towards God (thus hoping for the Messiah's arrival) gave a deep perception to this suffering and allowed it to be overcome more easily.

The Inquisition was a good intermediary for the performance and compliance of these sufferings, the tool that the Ca holic Monarchs used to homogenize Spain. Their origin dates back to the beginning of the 12th century, when Pope Innocence III created it to repress the Albigensians, Cathars or Patharines, denominated Manichean and the poor Waldensians of Lyon and other very popular heretics of the time in France Midi and North of Spain and Italy. It was established in Castile in 1480, by Papal Bull, decree issued on November 10, 1478. It was organized "as a necessary element for Spain to perform its mission and achieve political union cemented on the religious unity of its people".[75] It was requested formally for the fight against Catholic apostles of Jewish origin.

The American Inquisition tribunals were more zealous in their hunt for heretics and were crueler in their punishment than the Spanish Inquisition itself, although their members were not always examples of high moral value.

When the first American diocese was erected, its head was granted the faculty of operating in questions pertinent to the purity of Catholic belief as special representative of the Holy Office by the Spanish General Inquisitor.

The two first bishops in Mexico, Fray Juan de Zumárraga and Montúfar were invested with the power conferred to them in the Verona Concilium to judge those people suspicious of heresy.

There were three textbooks which the Inquisition in New Spain used to adapt its rulings: that of Torquemada (compilation of the instructions of the Holy Office of the Holy Inquisition). One of Valdés: "Ordinances of Toledo" and the formulary of García, secretary of the Council, entitled "Order that is commonly kept at the Holy Office of the Inquisition about processing causes treated within it, according to that which is provided by the old and new instructions."[76]

When the Inquisition was established in New Spain, Moya de Contreras was given precise instructions about the proceedings. Ever since 1535, the Spanish General Inquisitor, Alfonso Manrique, Archbishop of Toledo, issued the title of Apostolic Inquisitor to the bishop of Mexico, Fray Juan de Zumárraga.

What is horrifying about the methods used by the Inquisition is, doubtlessly, torture and death by fire. The Inquisition always tried to save face and civil judges were the ones who dictated the death sentences according to common law and so it was performed.

---

[75] Jiménez Rueda, J., *Historia de...,* p. 95.
[76] Medina, J. Toribio, *op. cit.,* p. 10.

From its very establishment, the Inquisition determined to have a political and religious goal. The monarchs were able to make use of the Inquisition as a tool directed to procure greater concentration of authority through the assimilation of various groups of populations and diverse religions.

The Inquisition did not pride itself with being merciful, kind, of love of humanity and the ardent and disinterested desire of saving heretics from eternal death and good Christians from the dire infection of that spiritual leprosy that was contracted through a word, a greeting and even through charity, when a Catholic broke bread or gave haven to some persecuted criminal as proclaimed by the Holy Office.

The secret was the soul, nothing need be known or revealed. From the moment when the Apostolic Inquisitor took possession of his position until the time when the accused left the prison, everyone without exception swore to keep all doings secret.

This secret made it almost impossible to have a defense and the accused was always "in the dark", trying to guess what he was accused of, who his accuser was, who the witnesses against him were, what was demanded of him and what did they suppose he would say in his defense or against others.

People were denounced to the Holy Office in various ways: anonymously or through a person who came voluntarily to declare against somebody, by accusations of the attorney himself, etc. Upon being arrested, all their assets were confiscated. They began by examining him in the matter of religion and he was asked if he knew the reason for his detention. The accused had to remain rigorously isolated without communicating with anybody until he was sentenced. He submitted to a number of different torments until he confessed his sins and, at the same time, informed against other people. He was never told what the judges really wanted to know, so the victim had to guess in the middle of his pain what was demanded of him.

Sometimes, torture was suspended because the accused began to talk, but other times, the victim said nothing because of his fortitude or because he was able to withstand martyrdom.

In those cases they went from the rack to water torture, "it consisted on laying the accused on the same rack and by means of a rag, to have him drink an amount of water, but the rag was placed in such a way that one end was inside the mouth all the way to the throat, producing insufferable anxiety and pain in the victim".[77] If, in spite of such torture, the accused did not confess they would say that "he had overcome torture" and he was recalled again later. They wrote down that the accused had suffered no wounds.

Torture was different in every region as well as the methods for applying it.

Sentence was of absolution when the victim was able to prove his innocence or when the attorney who was the accuser could not prove the person's guilt. If the accused confessed and demonstrated his repentance, sentence was of reconciliation in which case the statement where he confessed, retracted his sins, hated the crimes and promised to remedy them was read publicly in the Auto-da-fe; however, these people lost their assets forever and were condemned to jail for perpetuity. If the sentence was of relaxation, the sentence was to give the victim up to the secular arm for punishment, always asking for mercy towards him. Sometimes this meant the stake, whether he was burned alive or garroted first. This last sentence passed his infamy to all coming generations, that is, his children and grandchildren.

But any of the other sentences also meant a stigma within the family. When the sentence was against a person already dead, he was burned in effigy and his assets were confiscated regardless; the same was done if he were not to be found anywhere.

The sentenced and the convicted went out with the insignia of their crime, usually a candle, cord, shell and sambenito. The candle was made of green

---

[77] Jiménez Rueda, J., commentary to Medina's book, *op. cit.,* p. 24.

wax, the cord was tied around the neck, the shell was a type of miter of the same color as the sambenito; this was a yellow sleeveless jacket that at the beginning looked like a tunic and eventually became a wide scapular or cape that came down slightly below the waistline.

The sambenito had to have various drawings according to the sentence dictated: with tongues of fire surrounding him – symbol that the victim would be burned alive – and with a devil as symbol that they would finish off the soul of the accused. The sambenitos of those who died or escaped were placed in churches and if they were lost or destroyed a Royal Decree and Accepted Letters of the Inquisition Council would take care to have them replaced.

The jails of the Holy Office were: the Secret, where the isolated prisoners remained until a definite sentence had been pronounced and the Perpetual or merciful one, where those who had already been condemned were placed; there, they were allowed to work at some art or job to earn a living and, in some cases, they were permitted to go out and beg for food by alms; others complied with their jail sentence wearing perpetual garments in the home particularly in those small towns where there wasn't room enough for so many convicts.

One of the most important tasks the monarchs requested the inquisitors to do was to search for forbidden books. The commissaries of the Holy Office searched all incoming vessels meticulously as well as printing presses and bookshops. They feared that any of those books filled with either Lutheran or Jewish ideas would enter the New World.

The Inquisition of New Spain celebrated magnificent and sumptuous Autos-da-fe. The stands were erected so that all the people could observe the ceremonies, one for the viceroy and his entourage, another for the audience, for the ecclesiastic and secular chapters, for the university, for distinguished families and one for the general public.

The viceroy's stand was usually next to some building that was richly furnished and bridges were placed towards a window on the upper story so that the important people would be able to have refreshments served and even a room for the viceroy to rest.

Near the building of the Holy Office a platform was set up for the magistrate who dictated the sentence of the "relaxed" (to be executed); they would listen to the sentence of the Inquisition. From there, the retinue of the condemned, including the statues of those to be executed in effigy or the bones of those who had been "relaxed", was led towards the "quemadero" (area for burning) that occupied the Western edge of the park nowadays called Alameda where executions were held.

If ever the converts in the New World expected that the distance from their previous life and the newly begun one would allow them to live in tolerance without being insulted with injurious names as a memory of their ascendance or being imprisoned, they were absolutely wrong because they found "the same furious contempt with the same relentless passion."

When somebody's condition as new Christian was found out, without any other indication about his or his ancestors' conversion whether sincere or not, he was immediately considered a Judaizer. The family was mercilessly spied upon and put under a ruthless lens to analyze their every act; information was given as to their whereabouts, the people they kept ties with, the food they ate (information also contributed by slaves and servants). The knowledge that some citizens washed their hands before sitting down to eat made them wonder whether they should accuse them before the tribunal. And if by chance, a Portuguese went past a symbol representing the Catholic religion without donning off his hat that was cause enough to be accused as Judaizer and heretic before the Holy Office.

All these insignificant details allowed the Holy Office to have a thorough file of suspicious people in the matter of faith.

Life for people who were considered Judaizers and heretics was made almost impossible because they were mocked, reviled and objects of contempt, so that even a vulgar criminal was considered above any of them. They were pointed out and scorned wherever they went.

The rift opening between Judaizer converts and Castilian society surrounding them became so deep that nothing seemed to narrow it, not even family ties were strong enough to lay a bridge between two opposing ideologies that struggled desperately to predominate.

The Holy Office reigned throughout Hispanic America controlling the religious behavior of all its inhabitants whether white, (mestizo) mixed white and Spanish, black or mulatto. Only the Indians, whose mental maturity was in question, were exempt from its yoke.

In Mexico, the Inquisition was suppressed for the first time in 1813, as consequence of a decree of the Cádiz courts of that year and reestablished in 1815 when King Ferdinand VII returned to the Spanish throne. It was definitely abolished when Spanish absolutism was defeated.

Inquisitorial proceedings, models of idealism and perseverance

How many Judaizers were processed and had the opportunity for martyrdom? We must recall that the area of the Inquisition in the Archivo General de la Nación is made up of 1557 volumes in which there are a huge number of processes of Crypto-Jews that took place in New Spain.

Each one of them deserves a separate study. We have chosen a few of the accused whose lives were significant, whether because of the time, age, social position, sex, etc. but mostly because of their devotion and love to the "dead Law of Moysen". Most of the processes show incredible idealism and fidelity towards Jewish religion.

The illiterate Francisco Millán

We have called Millán illiterate, because although he was a good Jew, he could not read or write, something very unusual among the population of Judeo-Spanish origin.

Francisco was originally from the kingdom of Castile, from Villa de Huesca. His father had been born in Contrera and his mother in Costatina; both were reconciled by the Holy Office in Spain and had left him an orphan at a tender age. Although he was practically illiterate, he knew the Jewish traditions and had been circumcised. After his parents' death he lived in Seville and later in Portugal where he had friends and relatives of his same creed. Pretty soon he began buying and selling wine, trade that he continued exercising on his arrival in America.

In Spain he married Isabel Sánchez, originally from Jerez de la Frontera, with whom he had six children, three boys and three girls who were still in the peninsula when he was processed in the New World.

Millán, the type of Jew of the lower social strata, bereft of instruction, decided to arrive in America to make his fortune so he could later bring his family. He arrived in Mexico City in 1536 (date in which we understand life in the Colony was still difficult), and he tried to establish himself by going back to his old trade as tavern keeper.

In spite of his lack of culture, he continued his Judaic practices in the New World. Thanks to his occupation he soon met all his fellow Jews who resided in the Colony and who came to him to buy Sabbath wine and chat about daily life and their difficulties.

In spite of every Royal Decree and Edict about the ban of converts going to the Indies, they tended to do so easily, particularly at the beginning before the Tribunal began functioning officially.

Millán was denounced to the Inquisition because it seems an Indian servant and concubine told a story to a wine dealer. She said that he had flagellated an image of Christ, had broken two crosses and had demanded from the servant to return some money she had stolen.

Millán had sold the slave a month before being accused to the Inquisitor Fray Juan de Zumárraga. This slave had been taken first to Oaxaca and on to Peru, so her testimony could not be obtained.

The case of Francisco Millán is very interesting because it shows Zumárraga exercising the office of inquisitor in all its breadth. The man was accused of suspicion of being a Jew and of having whipped an image of Christ. He was judged with all the weight of the Law although the Inquisition was not officially installed until 1571. He was tortured repeatedly so he would confess to his guilt.

The accused declared on December 24, 1538 that he didn't remember his parents, because when he was four years old he had been taken from his native city to Seville as an orphan; that somebody had placed him with a man called Diego de Sevilla, who manufactured socks. In a later statement he added that five years earlier, while being in Lisbon, in the kingdom of Portugal, a Spaniard had told him that he had known his parents who were of Jewish origin just like him, and having inquired from Millán whether he had been baptized, he had answered he didn't know, so he had since wondered whether or not he had ever been baptized.

He also said that during the last Lent he had eaten meat without a physician's prescription because he didn't feel well and that he had once gone to Azamor to sell some material and he brought from there a Moorish woman and had carnal relations with her knowing full well that she wasn't a Christian.

In the following statements, the prisoner confessed new sins, true or false, but as the process advanced and he was submitted to torture, he referred to Albar Pérez as well as to Alvaro Mateos as good Jews like he was. He later added the names of Carmona, Astorga, Redondo, Alonso de Cisneros, Alonso de Pardo, de Córdoba, someone by the name of López, another whose last name was Morón, etc. He was tortured by cord lacerations on hands and feet.

From Millán's process we can see the first community efforts of Jews in New Spain and that even at such an early time in Colonial history there were a good number of them.

He testified before Bishop Zumárraga, that, in general, Jews knew one another and they sometimes ate together observing food laws. Some of them, including his parents, had worn a sambenito in Spain.

In one of the interrogations, Millán added that since the interview with the man who had told him that his parents were Jewish, he had considered himself Jewish as well but he wouldn't confess it before the Tribunal as penance, but he had not participated in rites or Jewish ceremonies, had never seen one and didn't know of them. This was patently false, but fear of consequences was very great.

As torture persisted, he was forced to confess that his parents were Jewish, finding out and certifying it in Lisbon when he was twenty years old, that he was Jewish, that the man who told him had taken him to his house where they ate and drank together and he had met other Jews and had gladly watched their ceremonies from the door of the synagogue which he did not dare enter for fear of being discovered by Christians and he said that "when he went to church it was to comply with people".

All this was amazing naiveté: his Judaism was real even though he had only learned of it at twenty. Here we have a number of questions: if he was raised and educated as a Christian and only found out his religion at twenty, knowing that being Jewish would bring so many problems upon him, why did he enjoy being it and watching the ceremonies only from outside the synagogue? Why did he go back to Judaism upon arriving in New Spain where only those with blood purity could go while he was able to live as an old Christian?

From the Inquisition jail he sent a letter to the Inquisitor in which he confessed to having lived as a Jew and talked about the man who had helped him keep the Law of Moses saying: "this man of Lisbon knew my parents as Jews, he told me to keep said Jewish law that was a better law than that of Christians and to eat and drink what was good and whatever evil I could do to Christians I should do and why should I go to church when Jewish law was better than Christian law; that I shouldn't listen to things in church because the Messiah had still not arrived, and he also told me he ate unleavened bread which he used to eat in Portugal, in Lisbon and in Castile they ate it. So I was in Jewish homes and I ate and drank with them and enjoyed everything they did in Portugal and I kept Sabbath like other Jews did and in Lisbon I was in homes of Jews where we wore something on the head and another Jew who knew about the Law of Moysen and I did as the other Jews did with my chapel on my head but I did not understand the work they were reading and also, I have had the habit in Castile of not bringing home meat unless it was clean although they told my wife that the meat was exposed and they said there was devil in the meat so they said, and I didn't take out the nerve from the meat so she should not understand that I was Jewish and she said she did not do it and she also did many Jewish things that I don't have in my memory, I also say that she fasted all Jewish fasts and every Friday she would have clean candlesticks for Saturday, she kept it and did nothing and I also remember, your reverend highness, that here in this land and remembering the Law of the Jews I did in Castile...."

Many facts can be deduced about the previous letter about Jewish habits performed by all converts, the way they did them, the naiveté of the description, his faith in what he considered correct and true in spite of his lack of culture. But if Millán said he did not know how to read or write, then who wrote the letter for him? Was it a confession before a scribe? At the end of the letter there is neither signature, not Millán's nor the scribe's.

The handwriting appearing in that letter is different from the one of the person writing the rest of the process. Was it Millán who wrote it himself? Then, why did he lie saying that he could not read and write? Was he really illiterate?

Francisco Millán, whether illiterate or not, was a convert faithful to his religion and although he was one of the first immigrants of Jewish origin into New Spain, having gone through an enormous number of obstacles and inconveniences, he continued performing all Jewish rites and ceremonies.

Fear made him confess many things and leave others in doubt; one of them is his wife's origin that obviously was Jewish but he did not want her to fall into the hands of the Holy Office in Spain. The letter shows that she was one herself, when he mentions the candlesticks for Sabbath and cooking on Friday so as to rest the next day.

All his assets were confiscated and everything was put on sale (there is a list of his possessions and their prices in the process). His confession and sentence were read in the presence of Bishop Fray Juan de Zumárraga and Viceroy Antonio de Mendoza. The sentence said:

"We find that we must condemn and we condemn said Francisco Millán that on Sunday or holiday indicated by us he be taken out of the house of the Holy Office and taken bodily to the great church of this city with a candle in his hand and he be placed on a high catafalque and while major mass is going on he should be there in body with the lit candle on his extended hand and uncovered head and together he must abjure and loathe and retract all his errors and Jewish life as he has confessed and make him in which case he is required of no more returning to said errors or Jewish life and of not believing and keeping the Holy Catholic faith and of defending it according to what he is ordered and sent and while the sermon he should sit and while the Holy Sacrament is reached until it is consumed he must be on his knees and afterwards until the mass is over he should stand and more we condemn him to wear a sambenito, over all his clothes as is the use and habit which he must wear on top of all his clothes every time he goes out of his home and when he is in it he must wear it on top of his frock which he cannot take off without license from his majesty or the lord inquisitors residing in the city of Seville, and we order that in the first vessel that goes from these parts to the kingdoms of Castile he should go to those kingdoms exiled and he should not come back to these parts and he should present himself before said inquisitors with all the process of his cause and he should not come back to any part of the Indies, nor the Islands under the pain of being imposed. We condemn him to the loss of all his goods applied to the treasury of his majesty of this Holy Office."

Fray Juan de Zumárraga (Bishop Apostolic Inquisitor)

Millán's requirement of exile included taking the first boat going to Spain. In 1539 he was seen in Taxco begging for alms wearing the sambenito. Later on, he was spotted in Zultepec and in Toluca still begging.

A Sambenito and a Relajado

The idealist Luis de Carvajal el Mozo

"Blessed are the martyrs who are the faithful and real Jews who die for their faith, whom the princes that persecute them without cause unjustly call Judaizer Heretics; because Judaizing is not heresy, but rather doing what the Lord Our God commands us". This was written by Luis de Carvajal el Mozo or Joseph Lumbroso, as he called himself in the testament, he asked permission to write before perishing at the stake.

He concluded this letter offering his life and that of his family to Almighty God, the God of Israel saying: "….And as I have a mother and five sisters endangered, even if I had a thousand, I would give as much for the faith of each one of God's Holy Commandments. I gladly finish off the sayings of my present life, bringing living faith in Your divine hope of salvation through Your infinite mercy and of resuscitating when Your holy will shall be complied, in the company of our Holy Fathers Abraham, Isaac and Jacob and their faithful children, for whose holy love I beg You humbly to confirm and don't abandon me and do please send in my aid and defense that Angel Michael, our prince, with his holy angelic army, to help me preserve and die in Your holy faith and he should free me from the hands and temptations of the enemy."

This young idealist has been given a number of designations. He has been called mystic, illuminated, luminous, etc. and all of them agree perfectly with his personality. His life and that of his family faithfully reflect the life of Judaizers in colonial times.

This endurable expectation of a second life, that of honorable fame, the eagerness of survival dominating Judeo-Spaniards appeared in their religion in the purest and fullest sense. The Spanish saying "For honor, set down your life and set down both honor and life for your God" was very common.

Nothing better to judge the strength of the convictions and the spiritual power of Luis de Carvajal than his religious statement in writing in the form of testament that he delivered on September 12, 1596 (three months before dying) to the Inquisitor Dr. Lobo Guerrero, in the presence of his lawyer Canon Dr. Dionisio de Ribera Flores, when his sentence was read out to him.

His testament ends with the following words: "Give me grace my God and my Lord, in the eyes of those who keep me captive, so that in this kingdom and all those on this earth they should see and know that You are our God and that Your high and sanctified name is *Adonai*, that is invoked in truth in Israel and in His descendants, that I commend this soul that You gave me in Your very holy hands, protesting not changing my faith until death."[78]

Luis de Carvajal el Mozo went through two processes. There are few among the accused to show such solid conviction in the truth of a religion, deeper faith in the kindness of the same, more fervent mysticism when

---

[78] Publications of the A.G.N.M., Vol. XXVIII, *Procesos de Luis de Carvajal el Mozo,* Talleres Gráficos de la Nación, Mexico, 1935, p. 418.

confessing it and more pervading eagerness to sacrifice his life in its behalf, in the ideal.

Since the first process Luis declared having had celestial visions. His appellate of Joseph Lumbroso appears in the first process when he says: "That Lumbroso took for a dream that he dreamed being a prisoner in this jail now five years and it was that he dreamt that there was a flask full of a very precious liquor, encased in a sheath like a hat and that God told Solomon: Take a spoonful of this liquor and put it in the mouth of this good boy; …. that dream was a fire that God desired to give him so he would keep the Law of Moses and would understand the Holy Writings."[79]

Ever since he had that dream or revelation in which he saw that God himself had ordered to have the divine elixir of wisdom poured into his mouth in the secret jails of the Holy Office, he underwent a complete transformation and not only changed his name but he lost all fear and began to make active propaganda about his faith within the prison with Fray Francisco Ruiz de Luna and later when he was outside, in any occasion that presented itself.

Luis was convinced that God had made prodigious miracles for him and his family, showing mercy and demonstrating special inclination towards them. His fanaticism and a relentless rancor towards his persecutors only increased his love of the "Dead Law of Moses."

In spite of the many dangers that he and his family had suffered, he did not become more prudent; his fanaticism led him to put into effect the greatest risks being absolutely careless about praising and commending his creed and celebrating certain rites even in front of people he had just met.

The Carvajal home became "a significant Israelite center, a type of synagogue and place of refuge of Jews and Judaizers."[80]

---

[79] *Ibidem,* p. 234.
[80] Toro, Alfonso, *La Familia Carvajal.* Historic study about the Jews and the Inquisition of New Spain in the 16th century. Based on original documents mostly

All the members of the Carvajal family lived in a state of perpetual overexcitement caused mostly by the fasts and religious practices they kept. Thus, they constantly had dreams and visions that they interpreted as signs which God sent to favor them.

In his process, Luis said that his brother Balthazar had also changed his name for that of David. He always persisted in stating that the true Law was the one Moses granted the Jewish people and that it was the basis of their belief. These were the foundations:

1. This Law had been given to the Jews by the God Our Lord and it was predicated by Christians and they believe and guard the commandments of said Law.

2. If in some time there would arise among us a prophet or dreamer and this person would say that he has seen my visions and he would say and testify with miracles and would tell you to go away from my law from right to left hand, don't believe him, but you will keep in my law, because this is the temptation that I send you so it will be patent whether you love me.

3. "To see palpably complied with the curses that the Lord Our God prophesied through Moses on the Jews and over transgressors of the law, as is written in Deuteronomy, chapter twenty eight.

Luis was convinced that the sins committed by the children of Israel had caused them to be scattered in exile. Only through great suffering and total devotion would God forgive the people the sins perpetrated. And only after everybody repented and suffered for the Law, would God send the Messiah.

So he never lost faith and hope and he was able to infuse it onto the rest. When he was imprisoned by the Tribunal together with his mother and sisters, he tried to console them at every moment. Thus, he would send them

inedited that are kept in the Archivo General de la Nación of Mexico City. 2 Vols. Mexico, Ed. Patria, 1944, ils. facs., Vol. I, p. 97.

words of comfort written in the banana peels or avocado seeds of his breakfast saying: "Joy, joy because *Adonai's* angels and saints in Paradise expect my blessed martyrs of *Adonai.* I though of going alone, my blessed one, send me a sign of whether you are by yourself or not..."[81]

These words help explain the mysticism characteristic of the time of Luis de Carvajal el Mozo, not only among Hispano-Jews but among all Spaniards.

His conviction and fervor encouraged his mother and sisters with such tender words that they can move even unbelievers. He compared them with Biblical women to raise their spirit: "Souls of my heart, blessed of *Adonai, my God,* He visits you and comforts you in your tribulation and courage, courage, courage like Deborah, Yael and Judith; faith like Sarah, your Saintly Mother, zeal like Salome, saint martyr, prayer, prayer because you are awaited in Paradise with the crown; rejoice, rejoice, joy, joy, rejoice that you go like Saba to see the King of Angels, to enjoy His beauty and wisdom; joy hallelujah."[82]

Luis had been born in Villa de Benaventes in a Jewish home where he spent his first years. Later he went to live with his parents in Medina del Campo; there he studied, besides Latin and rhetoric, the Mosaic religion. His family was, like so many others, a family of converts that continued keeping the Jewish religion. They lived on the Portuguese border where it was easy to go to Spain if they so desired or to New Spain.

When his uncle received a permit to take one hundred families to New Spain to settle the New Kingdom of Leon, they decided to accompany him because this opportunity offered them a comfortable life and a new horizon to develop more freely. Although Luis de Carvajal el Viejo (the old) was really a "new Christian", perhaps he was aware that his relatives continued practicing Judaism, but he never mentioned it. He was sure that in America they would forget everything and be good Christians just like he was. His

---

[81] Publications, *op. cit,* p. 172.
[82] *Ibidem,* p. 177.

wife, Guiomar, fervent Jewess, decided not to go with him to America because she was unable to convince him to return to Judaism.

A few years after having arrived in New Spain, Luis de Carvajal el Viejo began facing some problems because of religious matters; the nephew who would inherit him was disinherited. So the latter began to seek his fortune elsewhere. He arrived with his father in Mexico who continued teaching him the Law of Moses. The father would say that "this was the true Law, the one that should be believed, because it had been given by God Himself and written with His finger on the tablets that He gave Moses, coming down from Heaven to give them."[83]

The young man accepted the Law of Moses as the only and true one, conscious of the dangers that this implied. To perform the pact with God he circumcised himself, running the risk of losing his life.

His father taught him to keep the Sabbath, "since Friday at sunset till Saturday night, not doing any type of work, wearing clean shirts, no more and no less than Christians keep Sundays, and this in memory of the world's creation when God, after He created everything, had rested on the seventh day, in which He should be praised, with psalms of glory and in that day no fire should be lit nor anything eaten except for what had been cooked the Friday before."[84]

While he was in Pánuco, he was able to buy a Bible from the vicar Juan Rodríguez, cleric who was very useful for his learning. In spite of the fact that Rodríguez de Mathos, his father, died when he was about 17 years old, Luis never forgot his teachings. His life was wrapped in a veil of mysticism. He never ceased keeping the food laws or fasting when it was necessary.

As a man well adapted to colonial life, he knew a great part of the territory of New Spain because he sold his merchandise from one end to another. In the Great Day of Atonement, he always tried to be with his

---

[83] *Ibidem,* p. 46.
[84] *Ibidem,* p. 47.

mother and sisters. In Passover, he used to read out loud passages from Exodus that describe the exit of the Jews from Egypt.

He felt that he belonged to the chosen people and he confessed it as such in his first process to the inquisitors that questioned him; he said that his father had taught him that "he and I and those that keep the Law of Moses are the people chosen by God, descendants of the Israelites and that all of those descendants of the Jewish people, descend from Abraham, Isaac and Jacob."[85]

Just like in many convert families, Luis had a brother who was a Franciscan friar called Fray Gaspar de Carvajal. He knew little about his family's beliefs but he probably suspected something because Luis and Balthazar had had some talks with him about religion without ever confessing to being Judaizers.

The sad fate of their uncle, in spite of being a good Christian, put them all on the alert. After having jailed him for political reasons, Luis' sister was imprisoned and thereafter her mother and the other sisters. Balthazar and Miguel managed to escape. In his first process, Luis el Mozo confessed his Judaism after a number of sessions. He narrated the way they had arrived in New Spain going from Medina del Campo towards Seville, passing through Carmona and from there embarking with the uncle for America.

Despite the great fear that the Holy Office and its inquisitors inspired, he did not cease with his religious practices. On January 26, 1590 they found a paper that contained some sonnets dedicated to the Lord, asking forgiveness for sins committed:

> Receive my fast in penitence,
>
> Lord of every evil I have committed;
>
> Don't allow your mercy to be missing
>
> Because you see how anxiously I beg for it;

---

[85] *Ibidem,* p. 56.

I will extol your utter omnipotence,

Your name will be magnified

And, Lord, don't give me what I do not deserve,

Because I shudder just thinking.

If I have gravely offended you

It was for lack of understanding

For which I feel penitent

My thoughts go from here to there

I regret having disobeyed You,

You well know, Lord of the Heavens,

Because I know You shelter me

With Your merciful, sweet and soft face.

I confess I am not satisfied

Of my own work nor do I understand

If it is enough to free me from this bitter brew,

Because I don't pretend to work well;

Lord, take us out of this lake,

In which I always fear

That lacking this pardon

We shall dare not commit a sin.

The Lord does not desire our praise

Because He has need of it,

When we cannot increase it

Because He is immense in His Majesty

And he does not command our fasts

Because He desires something from us,

But because He loves us so much

That he desires that we love Him.

He wants and desires our salvation

And we shall enjoy His holy glory,

Which we cannot reach

If we don't remember his Holy Law;

Let us grant the God we have

His grace, softness and faithful victory,

So that away from the vices

We shall return to our good exercises.

Their fear of God was greater than the fear of the inquisitors; in spite of the physical pain suffered by torture, suffering would be worse when the time came to face the Lord of Heaven.

I have sinned, Oh Lord, but not for having sinned
Do I take leave of Your love and mercy;
I fear being punished because of my guilt
And I hope in Your kindness to be forgiven;
I fear that You have awaited for me
In my ingratitude to be loathed
And it increases my sins
When You are so worthy of being loved;

If not for You, what would become of me
And me, without You, who would free me
If Your hand, grace would not grant,
And if not I, Oh Lord, who would not love You?
And if not You, Oh Lord, who would suffer for me?
And You, without You, Oh Lord, who would take me?[86]

Luis de Carvajal eventually asked for forgiveness before the inquisitors for having believed in the Law of Moses; perhaps this, as well as his youth, led to his sentence being of absolution. When the sentence was read to him he confessed "that he had been in the belief of said Law of Moses, believing that he would be saved through it and in his guard, performing the rites and ceremonies that he had confessed…. and he had kept it in prison, not doing any exterior thing besides praying to God on Saturdays, psalms of praise without Glory Patri, for not confessing the persons of Jesus Christ keeping them as feast in whatever he could."[87]

His repentance seemed sincere to the lord inquisitors. "Heedful that said Luis de Carvajal, in the confessions made previously, showed signs of contrition and repentance, asking Our Lord God forgiveness for his crimes and from us penitence with mercy, protesting that from here onwards he wanted to live and die in Our Holy Catholic Church and he was ready to comply with any penitence that we would impose on him…. we admit him to be reconciled and we order that in penitence of this our sentence he shall come out to listen to it in this edict with the other penitents in body, without belt or bonnet, with a penitential frock of yellow cloth, with two red wings of Saint Andrew and a wax candle in his hands where it will be read and there publicly he shall abjure of said errors that he has confessed to us and any other king of heresy or apostasy; and once having abjured we order him to be absolved and we absolve any excommunication sentence in which for reason

---

86 *Vid.* Documentary appendix.
87 Publications, *op. cit.,* pp. 102-103.

of the previous he had fallen into or incurred and we unite him to reincorporate to the guild and union of the Holy Mother Catholic Church, and we restitute him to participate in the Holy Sacraments and communion of the faithful and Catholic Christians of it and we condemn him to jail and perpetual habit, which he will guard and comply in the monastery or part or place that we shall indicate so that there he shall serve and be instructed and confirmed in the things of Our Holy Catholic Faith and that said habit he shall wear publicly, on top of all his garments and he shall guard and comply with the other spiritual penitence that we shall declare; and we declare that said person shall be rendered unfit and incapable of getting or having dignities nor public office nor of honor and series descended of the other things that from common right laws and pragmatics of these kingdoms and instructions of the Holy Office of the Inquisition to such unfit persons are forbidden."[88]

The place where he had to execute his sentence was the Convalescent Hospital, ordering him to take care of the decent things and services that the administrator would indicate. His spiritual consolation was entrusted to Fray Mateo García, Knight Commander of the Order of Mercy.

Luis de Carvajal el Mozo spent several years there until October 20, 1594, when in an audience before the Tribunal, his penalty of using the sambenito was commuted, by paying a "pecuniary punishment of 325 ducats."

He knew he could not occupy important public positions or wear jewels or precious stones or silk, but he had to live like a real new Christian, because relapsing into Judaism meant death by burning.

As time went by, Luis became more and more absorbed in his beliefs, not caring whether he died in the sacred name of God (what in Hebrew is called *Kidush Hashem*).

The only way of saving his soul was believing in the Jewish religion that was the only and true one. During his second process not only did he boast of his beliefs, but he showed himself ready to die for them. His faith was so

---

[88] *Ibidem,* pp. 106-107.

firm and his enthusiasm for dying in it so great and alive that "it bordered on folly."[89]

When his accusation was read out, Luis de Carvajal el Mozo begged God to discover real heresies and that "by putting him in red hot fire it would a mystery for him to go and enjoy the eternal glory of the Lord Our God, according to how the blessed Eliezer, Salome and the seven holy Maccabee sons…"[90]

Letting himself be driven by his unquenchable faith, he looked with deep disgust upon his prison, torture and even death itself; he was sure he would be a martyr of his belief, martyrdom that would be rewarded by God in his eternal fortune. He took over the role of a real rabbi, stating from the Holy Scripture that the Messiah would arrive in the year 1600. God, from the top of Sinai, would send the redeemer to predicate the Law. And only He would be the one to forgive all the sins committed. Passionate in his belief, he was also fearful of torture. Under torture he confessed the names of other Judaizers that believed like he did that salvation would come in the Law of Moses; this did not mean cowardice or lack of moral courage, but martyrdom bordering on the unbearable made him talk.

From the number of people denounced by young Carvajal, we can infer about the great number of converts residing at the time in New Spain, performing almost every kind of trade and profession: merchants, teachers, lawyers, comics, tailors, shoemakers, even friars. All the names that appear in his process belong to fervent Jews who visited the church pretending a Christianity they did not profess.

Many times Luis protested saying that he would not "confess or denounce anybody even though they would cut him up in pieces that he would die in his Law". But torture ended up by defeating his will and he talked long and in great amounts. Through his confession before the inquisitors we can easily depict Jewish life in the colonial era. His attitude was that of a man deeply

---

[89] Toro, *La Familia*…., vol. II, p. 238.
[90] *Ibidem,* p. 238.

convinced of his belief, determined to suffer martyrdom joyfully for the triumph of faith, in spite of the fear he had of fire.

Did Luis de Carvajal el Mozo, also known as Joseph Lumbroso, convert as Fray Alonso de Contreras says in his story? It is not very probable. His living faith in the Law of Moses was the light of his existence.

He was Jewish until his last moments and he continued being Jewish. Even if he had converted a second before being lighting the fire, his conversion would not have been accepted as real not even by the inquisitors themselves.

His testament is a faithful testimony of his beliefs, what it meant for him to be Jewish, of having made a pact with the God of Israel through his circumcision.

The document says in the first part:

"Almighty and Sovereign Creator of heaven and earth, under whose will none of the things You created can resist, and without it men, birds, brute animals could not survive on earth; that if Your want and will did not sustain them and ordered the elements to be confused with the heavens, they would lose the natural course of movement, the whole earth would tremble, the hills and great mountains would fall, the seawater would cover the earth and no living thing would have any support and You, who in Your infinite kindness and mercy order and sustain everything, not because it is necessary for You, but for the common good and benefit of men, and from so much mercy and infinite compassion that You give them, I, the poorest and most miserable of all, I ask and beg You in alms that under the danger and peril of death that in honor of Your Holy Name and real Law I want to receive, do not abandon me, accept the poor life that You gave me in sacrifice, overlooking my innumerable sins, but at Your mercy and for this immortal soul that You created in Your image for eternal life, which I beg You to forgive and receive when it has gone out of this mortal body that ordering my testament and last will and definitely concluding I write and sign the religious truths that I believe and I protest dying in Your presence.

First of all I believe in one only real Almighty God, creator of heaven, earth and oceans and of all the things visible and invisible and I renege of the devil and all his prevarications.

"I believe that the Lord Our God and Universal Creator is one and no other... I believe that the Law of Lord Our God, that the Christians call dead of Moses, is life and endless..."[91]

"There is no doubt, says José Almoína, that we are in the presence of a mystical character, product both of secular inheritance as well as influenced by his time, and no wonder because Luis de Carvajal el Mozo was formed in his youth in the years of maximum expanse of Hispanic literature and the era when mystical authors were expanding throughout America."[92]

He was sentenced and relaxed to the Secular Arm with these words: "And so, accepting his confessions made in my favor and not more and affirming in my accusation, I ask Your Highness to be declared as true and my intention as well proven and said Luis de Carvajal as heretic, Judaizer, impenitent relapsed, Apostate of Our Catholic Faith, simulated having confessed in what he confessed at the time and before he was reconciled in this Holy Office; stubborn dogmatic and teacher of the Law of Moses, to be burned at the stake while alive in flames of fire, so that he be punished and be an example to others, his assets pronounced as confiscated and belonging to the Chamber and Treasury of His Majesty since the day in which he committed the crimes of heresy and apostasy of which I accuse him...."[93]

His conviction of saving his soul through the truth of the Law of Moses did not abandon him till the last moment. He was sentenced to die at the stake "in flames of fire", so he would serve as an example to others. He was

---

[91] *Vid.* Documental appendix

[92] Almoína, José, *op. cit.,* p. 92.

[93] Publications of the Archives, *op. cit.,* p. 272.

an example, but perhaps not the one the inquisitors wanted to present, but rather an example of fidelity, love and perseverance of an ideal of martyrdom.

The persistent Tomás Treviño de Sobremonte[*][94]

Tomás Treviño de Sobremonte, also known as Jerónimo Represa, was one of the most fervent Jews in the New World, of extraordinary frame of mind, impetuous hidalgo with an overwhelming pride.

He had escaped from Spain in 1611, under the alias of Jerónimo de Represa. He had studied Canon Law in the city of Salamanca but he abandoned his studies at its famous university at 16 (1609) to become a page "having killed a service companion for having called him a Jew."[95]

He arrived in America to make his fortune and get away from everything that had any relationship with the Holy Office, but he only deceived himself.

The hate with which the inquisitors refer to him is extraordinary. He is always called "perverse and treacherous Jew; feigner, simulator, execrable, criminal, filthy dog that returned to vomit and to lick the apostasy that his stomach had thrown out, Jew of the worst kind, etc...."

He was born Tomás Treviño in the city of Medina de Rioseco in Old Castile, son of Antonio Treviño de Sobremonte, originally from the same city of Medina de Rioseco and Leonor Martínez de Villagómez, originally from Cuenca de Campos. This woman was relaxed in effigy as Judaizer, by the Valladolid Inquisition just like her sister and cousin respectively Ana Sánchez de Guevara and Dr. Tomás Sánchez de Guevara as well as Jerónima Sánchez de Guevara, nun professing at the convent of the same city of

---

[94] A.G.N.M., R.I., T. XX. Exp. 5, Riva Palacio Lot, 1625, "Causa criminal contra Tomás Treviño de Sobremonte, natural de la ciudad de Medina de Rioseco, por judaizante".
[95] Lewin, *Los Judíos...*, p. 74.

Medina de Rioseco. His father was a merchant in that Spanish city. He spent the first years in New Spain going from one city to another, selling wares of all kinds.

In 1619, his brother was imprisoned by the Holy Office of Valladolid and after being tortured, he gave testimony about his family and this caused Tomás to be taken to the jail of the Inquisition.

The first years in Mexico were difficult until he was able to settle in the capital. He traveled very much and knew the territory and its inhabitants well. Since the first moment he made contact with his fellow Jews already living there, having great friendship and an affectionate relationship with most of them.

Treviño was an intelligent man, a fighter who would not rest until he got what he wanted. He soon made a small fortune and decided to open a store in the city of Oaxaca.

Since he was very young, his mother taught him to believe in the Law of Moses and to consider Jewish religion as the "good and true one". In the New World, Tomás continued with his Jewish practices in spite of it being very difficult.

He was accused the first time before the Holy Office in 1625 and imprisoned in the city of Oaxaca under the following accusation:

"Dr. Bartolomé González Soltero, Attorney of this Holy Office, in the best form and way according to right, having made the necessary solemn indications, criminally accused Tomás Treviño de Sobremonte, originally from Medina de Rioseco, merchant, residing in the city of Antequera, of the valley of Oaxaca, in this New Spain, where he was imprisoned here being present. And I say: that being said man Christian, baptized and confirmed and protesting being so and enjoying the privileges, immunities and exemptions that faithful and Catholic Christians enjoy and should enjoy, contravening the profession made at baptism, has done, said and committed, having been seen doing and saying and committing against whatever is predicated, followed and taught by the Holy Roman Church and Evangelic Law, simulating being real and Catholic Christian keeping and observing the dead Law of Moysen and its rites and ceremonies, living in it and firmly believing being saved in said Law.

> "I accuse him when being fourteen years old, in said town called Rioseco, having Leonor Martínez, mother of said accused, communicated and treated many things against our Holy Catholic Faith, in behalf and credit of the Law of Moysen, telling him to beware that what Christians adored were figures of sticks and metal and that Christ Our Lord was son of a carpenter and that the Law of Moysen was the real and true one that God had given it and in which he would be saved and so he had it in his heart and firmly believed and had it for certain and true, advising said Tomás Treviño de Sobremonte, her son that he should believe it with all his heart and keep it, as she did and said accused told her: that what she said seemed very good, giving entire faith and credit and effectively believed it firmly and had for certain, true and necessary for the salvation of souls said Law of Moysen changing to it and separating ever since from the faith and belief of the Holy Catholic Church."[96]

Tomás Treviño was an admirable Jew from infancy. In his first process, he confessed that his mother had taught him the Law of Moses since he was little and he had continued its rites and ceremonies; but when going to America he had left everything behind and had not gone back to the religion. He refused to confess that in New Spain he had followed the Law of Jesus Christ. All the witnesses who testified against him referred particularly to his life in the city of Medina de Rioseco and few talked about what he had done in Oaxaca as Judaizer.

---

[96] First process transcribed in the Bulletin of the A.G.N.M., T. IV, num. 2, pp. 449-450.

He was given a light sentence that stated "in conformity… for said man to go out in the first Auto-da-fe, with sambenito and be reconciled in form, his assets confiscated for the Chamber of the Treasury of His Majesty since the day when he began committing crimes of heresy and to be confined in perdurable jail with said sambenito for the time and space of a year and on Sundays and holidays he should listen to the great mass and sermon at the convent of Saint Domingo of this city with the other penitents; he should do so and comply, under pain of impenitent relapse."[97]

One month after being sentenced, he wrote to his inquisitors complaining of being sick and that the "cell where I find myself is so damp and full of water, that I am becoming deaf and my strength weakens which prevents me from doing something to earn my bread."[98]

His petition to be transferred to a hospital for six months was accepted and he was taken to the Hospital of the Abandoned with a permit to leave during the day to earn his living and go back to sleep at night.

On July 16 he was allowed to leave the sambenito and remain free by means of a payment to the Holy Office.

Tomás continued with Jewish practices and became the spiritual chief of the Crypto-Jewish community of New Spain that, by that time, was quite numerous, teaching it to follow the rites of the Law of Moses, hoping to get to see any day the dream of every American convert: "for the Messiah to appear on earth and for his chosen place to be precisely America". During his imprisonment he was circumcised by a fellow prisoner, Antonio Baez de Castelo Blanco, fervent Jew, whom he had instructed in the Law.

His mother, from the peninsula, informed him how his family had been jailed, particularly his brother Jerónimo Treviño, and she insisted that he should never forget his Judaism and to remember his prayers.

---

[97] Bulletin of the A.G.N.M., T. VI, num. 3, p. 463.
[98] Liebman, *Los Judíos…*, p. 294.

To You, great ineffable God,

To You, incomprehensible essence,

To You, firm and stable glory

To You, infallible Lord

To You, unchangeable Lord

To You, I confess and beg pardon and clemency;

If You see that I have offended You

My crimes and insolence

You do not owe me forgiveness

Do not look at me

And my iniquity and I live

Great God and look at You

And You will not enter into judgment

With me who offended You.

Much more than others I have sinned

So the world could blind me

Its pleasures I very much enjoyed

That so much of it I remembered

Of You I little recalled.[99]

Under torture he confessed having recited certain prayers to God, particularly while washing his hands:

Blessed be the powerful Adonai

That in Your teachings You taught me

To wash my mouth, hands and eyes

To praise and serve You

In laud and honor of the Lord

And in the Law of Moysen.[100]

---

[99] Bulletin of the Archive, T. VI, num. 4, pp. 581-582.
[100] *Ibidem,* p. 586.

Treviño was a good son and good pupil. His conviction in the truth of Jewish religion was absolute although he confessed in jail that he did that not knowing that he erred. We find the greatest proof of his Judaism in his second process. Such was his perseverance that he continued teaching the converts in New Spain after having been reconciled. After taking off the sambenito, his life continued its normal course, as if nothing had happened. Having to keep up appearances, he forgot certain things and would ride a horse, wore silk garments and precious jewels, things that were forbidden to any convert reconciled by the Holy Office.

In 1629, there was a complaint from "Doctor Bartolomé González Soltero, Attorney Promoter of this Holy Office against Tomás Treviño de Sobremonte, reconciled, about bearing arms"[101] He was accused of "bearing arms and using the other things that by said right are forbidden. Contravening the sentence that by Your Holiness was given and to the penitence imposed with great daring and contempt of this Holy Tribunal, he publicly bears arms and rides horses through the city and wears silk and fine clothing, by which he has committed great crime to be punished with the demonstration he deserves."

After the accusation he turned to the tribunal saying: "Illustrious mister Tomás Treviño de Sobremonte, resident of this city of Mexico: in the cause that through this tribunal was made, in which I was rendered unfit, which was sent to Spain, I have been habilitated by grant of Cardinal Antonio Zapata, General Inquisitor of all the kingdoms of His Majesty and the Supreme Inquisition, which I present at this Holy Tribunal. To Your Holiness I ask and beg admit it and grant me the mercy that through the Lord General Inquisitor has been granted to me. If I say that for having presented only today this habilitation and having borne a sword, I offer one hundred pesos for the expenses of this Holy Tribunal."[102]

---

[101] Bulletin of the A.G.N.M., T. VI, num. 4, p. 613.
[102] *Ibidem,* p. 617.

The decree or proposition of payment of one hundred pesos was accepted as was the fact that he could use all those garments forbidden to a man reconciled, descendant from Jews. "…We acquit with you said Tomás Treviño de Sobremonte and we habilitate you and give license and faculty that in spite of said sentence of reconciliation and other penalties imposed and executed in your person, you may bear arms, ride a horse, wear silk, gold and silver and other precious things, use and enjoy all other things arbitrarily forbidden to such reconciled and penitents of the Holy Office of the Inquisition, in all and any cities of the kingdoms and lands of His Majesty, and each and any of them in its district and jurisdiction that after this Royal Provision has its authentic transfer, signed and inscribed by Royal and public actuary that you showed them, shall guard and comply everything that is contained in it or any part of it shall put nor consent to set an embargo or any prevention. In testimony of which he orders to give and have given the present signed by our name, sealed with our seal and legalized by the King our Lord's Secretary and of his Council of the General Inquisition infra written in Madrid on May six of sixteen hundred and thirty two."

Cardinal Zapata (signature)

In 1629, he married María Gómez, another great Jewess, also processed for the crime of Judaizing. Her mother, Leonor Núñez, agreed to the marriage knowing how religious Tomás was.

The marriage was performed according to the Law of Moses. "And thus, on the day of the wedding, having invited to it many of his false belief and religion, he celebrated according to Jewish rites and ceremonies, covering his head while eating and before beginning all the other dishes, he ate a bun with bee's honey, arguing for it certain apocryphal story that he said was in the Scriptures that it must be done that way; slaughtering the hens to be served with a knife, his mother-in-law, Leonor Núñez, relaxed in person for being

Judaizer, relapsed in this auto, becoming through these ceremonies her son-in-law, saying three times when slaughtering them, turning her eyes to the East: blessed be the one who raised you for my sustenance and me for the earth and washing her hands with cold water, because it is a ceremony of the Jews when they bathe, or for fast or cleanliness, throw over the body three jars of cold water so they will not remain as they say, trefos or trefas, which is the same as soiled or dirty; and continuing this ceremony this accused, having been the first night with his wife, suspended the six following nights to see her on the seventh night, as observed by the Jews."[103]

Tomás prospered greatly after 1629 and because of a great flood in Mexico City moved out to the city of Guadalajara. He was merchant, traveler and producer of cochineal dye for export. When fleets arrived in Acapulco or Veracruz, he would buy wares coming from China, the Philippines or Spain.

He had six children with María, his wife: Rafael, the oldest was circumcised by his father when he was ten; he used a special knife and remained cloistered in his son's room until he healed. He soon began to teach him Jewish rites among which were the Monday and Thursday fasts.

In his store in Guadalajara he had a cross placed under the threshold so whoever entered stepped on it and if they were Jews they received a discount.

To deceive the servants about the reason for the fasts, he complained of liver trouble, so he had to abstain from food every so often.

He prayed four times a day. On Friday he would leave the candles to burn out by themselves so as not to desecrate the Sabbath. He knew the Jewish calendar, so he knew when the different feasts occurred.

The dietary laws were kept meticulously but when they had guests for dinner, to pretend, they put a piece of bacon in the soup. He constantly fasted. "The same in Mexico as in Guadalajara…. not reserving them even in roads and inns…it is not possible to determine the number, because except

---

[103] Bulletin of the Archives, T. VIII, num. 1, p. 162.

for that of Queen Esther and the Great Day, he did all of them with bathing, clean clothes and lighting candles…"

He performed the weekly fasts so that "….God would take him away from this land and towards somewhere where he could profess his law with security, having thought of going to France, Italy or Flanders… because when he fasted he seemed to be in clean and purified glory, to which said Treviño replied with false and Judaic devotion that He should remember him…"[104]

The syncretism between both religions is very clear in Tomás by the way he had of confessing; before doing it the Christian way he did it the Jewish way "cleaning beforehand all his body parts, wearing clean and very perfumed clothing and then he kneeled in a corner, the most remote in the house, his hands on the floor and his body so bent that he almost touched the floor and so he confessed heart and soul to the Almighty, begging forgiveness for everything he had done and remaining that way most of the day, fasting and after having spent other days in this Judaic, useless and superstitious confession he would go to Church where with fiction and complying he confessed…."[105]

His wife called him "Saint" because he knew as much about the Law as a rabbi. He taught her constantly so she could help him educate the children.

When María was reconciled by the Holy Office in 1635, she and Tomás together decided that he would refuse to receive her at home until the Tribunal would order it because "he had also been reconciled and they should not suspect of his relapse into Judaism."

In 1606 some of his books and merchandise were confiscated mentioning that Treviño, in spite of being reconciled, continued practicing Jewish ceremonies. These were never an obstacle to his having good and devoted

---

[104] *Ibidem,* num.4, p. 165.
[105] *Ibidem,* p. 166.

friends, even among old Christians. He was as well-adjusted to life in the Colony as any of them.

When he was fifty-two years old, he was arrested for the second time and taken to the secret jails of the Inquisition and relaxed, that is, burned alive in the great Auto-da-fe of April 11, 1649. He was not the only person thus punished, many were the Judaizers who came out in this Auto-da-fe (109); not all of them were burned at the stake, only 13 of them, but among them was Tomás Treviño de Sobremonte, the most obstinate of all.

There were many witnesses testifying against him (most of whom were prisoners) who talked in the torture chambers about his religious practices. A large number of them mentioned the wise teachings they had received from him in religious matters. They all referred to him as a sage.

In general, few of them said anything spontaneously; but when they were subjected to torture they would begin talking because what Tomás had instilled in them was never to denounce anybody.

His life as great erudite and knowledgeable in the Law of Moses doomed him every moment. He was accused of having incited both his wife and sister-in-law Isabel Núñez to denounce themselves before the Inquisition, because his mother-in-law and two other in-laws (Ana Gómez and Francisco López Blandón) were already in jail; of having been circumcised by one of their own, just like his son; of practicing continuous fasts, and to do them pleading "false headaches and not feeling hunger"; of not attending mass and confessing the Jewish way. It was said that when he finished eating dinner or supper together with Catholics, when greeted with good morning or good evening he did not answer "Blessed be the very holy Sacrament" but rather with "I kiss the hands of your grace". He was accused because his wife called him "Saint" and that in prison he used the Mexican language (probably referring to Aztec) to communicate with his brother-in-law, Francisco Blandón.

The night before his execution, he confessed very much of what he had kept to himself before the confessor: "the perverse apostate of our Holy Religion said that he was Jewish and that he wanted to die and live in the Law of Moses, the fathers and I being unable in spite of many arguments and clear demonstrations to induce him to the path of truth, although we convinced him, said the friar, of his error, many times this ignorant man responded with desperation, saying he died because of his money, denying his previous Judaism, when blaspheming he always said he was Jewish; in this battle the time indicated to go out to the Auto, that was Sunday of Quasimodo, April eleventh at five o'clock in the morning; not only was this beast already content with confessing the dead Law of Moses, but in his effrontery he would yell that we should follow him because his God was the true one...."[106]

During the walk of the procession towards the place where the Auto would be celebrated, "men, women and children, crying out loud for him to convert, praying the creed and other prayers out loud and he the most obdurate arrived at the stand where ministers and priests of every order tried once again to catechize him, and he still in his perfidy, without eating or drinking anything although it was offered to force him, he answered that he was fasting...."[107]

To the other Jews that went out together with him in that Auto, he encouraged them and told them "to be firm in their dead Law and having brought an old woman, his mother-in-law, who was also relaxed to hear her sentence, he said: 'Remember the mother of the Maccabees...' And after hearing the sentence he continued saying that he believed "only in the God of Israel."

On April 11, 1649, the Inquisition celebrated one of the most notable and magnificent of its Autos and, among others, judged and condemned Tomás Treviño de Sobremonte to death at the stake.

---

[106] Bulletin of the Archives, T. VIII, num. I, p. 156.
[107] *Ibidem.*

It said the following: "I decree, attentive to the guilt resulting against said Tomás Treviño de Sobremonte, whom I must condemn and I do condemn him to be taken through the public streets of this city, with a horseman on packsaddle beast and with the voice of town crier to manifest his crime, to the Tianguis of San Hipólito, in the part and place that for this is indicated, to be burned alive in flames of fire, until he has become ashes and no memory remains of him. And through this definitive sentence being so judged, I pronounce and send with a counselor to be immediately executed."

Don Jerónimo de Bañuelo y Estavilla

Don Francisco Hurtado Arciniega

"He went to the scaffold with the sambenito and shield of the condemned, without green cross in his hands because he refused to hold it, gag in his mouth because he emitted so many blasphemies that this was used so he could talk no more.

"Once in the hands of the authority he was mounted on a mule that bucked very much, he was changed to another one and then once again successively. The populace said that the animals refused to carry on their back such a Jewish dog. He was finally placed on a horse led by an Indian. The Indian exhorted Sobremonte to believe in 'God the Father, God the Son and God the Holy Spirit', but accompanied his words giving him terrible blows. The victim on horseback crossed the plaza, the portals, the streets of Plateros and San Francisco until they reached the stake located between the Convent of San Diego and the Alameda. He was tied to the execution pole. The multitude was immense; it filled all the avenues, the roofs of neighboring houses, the towers of the Church of San Diego and San Hipólito, the windows, all the tops of the trees of the Alameda."[108]

---

[108] González Obregón, Luis, *México Viejo, Época Colonial,* Mexico, Editorial Patria, 1959, p. 245.

The victim was burned alive in front of the eyes of the crowd without making a sound, not a moan. His process concluded with the following words:

"We have judged attentive to the autos and merits of said process, said promoter attorney having well proved and complied his accusation according to what was convenient to prove. We give and pronounce his intention for well proven, in consequence of which we must declare and do declare said Tomás Treviño de Sobremonte of having been and being heretic, apostate dogmatist rabbi abettor and of concealing heretics, counterfeit and simulated confidant, impenitent relapsed and thus of having fallen and incurred in sentence of excommunication and loss of all his assets, which we ordered to be applied and applied to the Royal Chamber and Treasury of His Majesty and his receptor in his name since the day and time when he began committing said crimes of heresy whose statement we reserve; and that we must relax and we do relax the person of said Tomás Treviño de Sobremonte to justice and the lay arm particularly to Don Jerónimo de Bañuelos, magistrate of this city and his deputy in said office, whom we beg and charge with great affection, as of right we best can, find themselves benignly and piously in it. And we declare the sons and daughters of said Tomás Treviño and his grandchildren on the masculine line to be rendered unfit so they may not have nor obtain benefits or dignities, nor trades whether ecclesiastic or lay, nor other public or honorable positions, nor can they carry on their persons gold, silver, pearls, precious jewels, nor corals, camlet silk, nor fine cloth, nor to go on horseback, nor bearing arms, nor exercising, nor using of other things that by common right, pragmatic laws of these kingdoms and instructions of the Holy Office to those similarly unfit are forbidden and thus our definite sentence judging we so pronounce and order in these writings and through them".

Juan Archbishop of Mexico

Dr. Don Francisco Estrada y Escobedo

Dr. Don Juan Sáenz de la Higuera y Amarilla

The maiden Violante Texoso

Violante Texoso, young woman eighteen years of age, was captured in the port of Veracruz where she lived with her aunts and other relatives, for practicing the dead Law of Moysen in 1645.

Her father was Don Rafael Gómez Texoso, born in the city of Valencia, Spain; he was a merchant who died shortly after arriving in New Spain. Her mother, Doña Leonor de Solier, was born already in the New World, in the city of Lima, Peru. She died when her daughter was very young, leaving her first in the care of the father and upon his death, in the hands of other relatives.

According to her process, we know that her grandparents were Pedro Gómez Texoso of Seville, trader who embarked towards the New World and died in the city of Lima. His wife, Doña Violante Rodríguez, Portuguese, met him in that city where they got married. When she became a widow, she went to the city of Veracruz where she died a very old woman. She was buried in the Main Church.

Violante never got to meet her maternal grandparents; she didn't even remember their names. She was an only daughter and when her parents died she was forced to live at some aunts who offered her shelter. She was born in the city of Lima where she was baptized, being daughter of converts. Her godfather was Duarte Rodríguez, married to her aunt Doña Clara Texoso. She studied in the city of Veracruz, at the School of the Jesuit Company, which means that she well knew the Catholic religion just like the rites and habits of the Jewish religion.

According to her confession, she knew how to read well but not to write. When she was imprisoned she was living with her aunts Doña Isabel Texoso, born in Valencia who was single and Doña Francisca Texoso, born in the city of Lima, also single, thirty years of age. Another person who lived with them was Doña Clara Texoso, younger than the two previously mentioned, originally from Lima, married to Duarte Rodríguez, Portuguese merchant; this couple had a ten years old son.

Doña Beatriz Texoso, also from Lima, had died as a maiden in the city of Veracruz and was buried also in the Main Church.

In her confession, the young woman mentioned having been born in the city of Lima, Peru, from where her father had taken her to New Spain, at a young age. When going to Veracruz with Rafael Gómez Texoso, her father, he had been accompanied by all his relatives. Together with them, there was another of her father's brothers, Captain Francisco Gómez Texoso, in whose house the girl lived when she became an orphan.

From the time of their arrival they began to have relations with people of their same type and habits. In her confession when Violante talked about the relationships they had with other people in the port of Veracruz, she referred to them as converts or new Christians that had gone to the New World just like they did.

Among those she mentioned there were Captain Serrano and his wife called Doña Mariana de Olivero, Doña Isabel de Oliva, wife of Francisco of the same surname; Melchor de Acosta, a blacksmith, who had arrived from Angola; Doña Juana Muñiz, wife of Jusepe de Medina; Doña Beatriz Medina, wife of Francisco Montelo and Doña Blanca, wife of Tomás Méndez.

The young woman recalled that when she was eight years old a woman who was a fervent Jewess came to her home (because it was always open to receive any fellow Jew who came to live in Veracruz) on her way to Cartagena and not having found passage at once, remained in the home of the Texosos during three months. Violante had to attend to the visitor, because upon arriving in Veracruz she had been ill of stomach trouble. The latter began teaching the girl the Law of Moses. She would tell her that she should not believe in the Law of Jesus Christ, because through the Law of Moses she could save her soul. "And the Law that she and many other people all together had followed and continued following and that one should believe in one sole God."

This woman taught her all the rites and traditions, instructed her about the fasts, on Mondays and Thursdays and on the great day of "Pardon", besides the fast of Queen Esther. She taught her how to extract the nerve from the meat to make it pure and always insisted that she not forget all that because in it lay her salvation.

They both shared the secret of being Jewish; the woman begged her not to tell anybody, "so she would not be burned". This was the way that Violante accepted the Law of Moses as the one and true Law".

In her confession, Violante accepted all the previous, she was convinced that that was the truth "trying since then to keep said Law of Moysen and to leave that of Our Lord Jesus Christ" and "she decided to believe in one sole God to save her soul and perform the fasts of said Law, to which she gave credit..."[109]

To dissimulate, she continued praying the Rosary to the Virgin, fasting in Lent, attending mass, she confessed and had communion. Most converts usually confused the ceremonies and mixed up one rite with others, sometimes forgetting which were really of Jewish origin and which were not.

The woman who instructed her recommended that she should try to find a man who professed the same creed to get married so she would be able to practice her Judaism freely.

Violante, in spite of her youth, kept the Jewish laws and traditions: "she kept the Sabbath, feeling sick, thinking as she really thought that by keeping said Law of Moysen she would be saved...."; besides, she kept the fasts as far as possible, "being without food nor drink the whole day and for the Negress who brought her a cup of chocolate in the morning should not notice

---

[109] All the quotations appearing in this case refer to T. LVII, exp. I, of the A.G.N.M., R.I.; because of lack of numbers of the pages, these cannot be cited.

that she did not drink it, would send her on an errand and in the meanwhile she gave the chocolate to some boys that were with her, and so as not to eat at midday together with some people she pretended to be sick of a toothache so she spent fasting till the evening when she ate fish and salad; very ordinary supper in said city of Veracruz…"

When being questioned by the inquisitors, she confessed under torture that she had concluded her decision "about which was the perfect Law, that should be followed and for God to forgive that woman that put her in such miserable and wretched state…"

When she was arrested, they also imprisoned her relatives who were in the jails next to hers. By means of fictitious names[110] they communicated with one another through the walls of the jail, and bribing the guards who brought them food, they sent each other letters of consolation.[111]

When communicating, they encouraged one another to continue and not to forget the commandments of the Law of Moses and to have the courage not to confess the guilt of others so as not to involve them. They all realized they would die, but God would compensate them with the glory of immortality, sending the Redeemer.

Bribes to the guards had been so effective that some knew to what degree others had confessed, "giving relation and news of what she had confessed in the audiences, to said people together and everything that happened there and because she had said nothing against them, although a certain lord Inquisitor urged her very, very much and that she should not look in that mirror nor say anything against herself, nor against anybody, conferring between themselves what they should say and confess, so as not to disagree in their

---

[110] *Vid.* Documentary appendix.

[111] She was called "Jazmin", others called themselves names such as: Celia, Malinchi, Valenciana, Capuli, Lirio, Azucena, Guacamaya, la Chocolatera, la Pecadora, la Tullida and many other names that she mentioned during her torture. This shows us the large number of people who fell into the hands of the Holy Office and the extensive colony of Judaizers who lived in the city of Veracruz.

sayings and depositions, nor do evil or damage some to others…" trying that the ones they knew were not yet in prison may save themselves and would not say "against many people, inhabitants of said city of Veracruz, accomplices in Judaism, deciding in concert in what they would confess and no more, cursing the persons of the lords Inquisitors, treating them with undue respect, because they urged them to discharge their conscience and to state thus all their crimes as well as said people together and one should say nothing about them although they would cut them up in pieces in torture, that they had courage and fortitude for it…"

These words of Violante by themselves depict the courage and the will to continue. She was determined to die at the stake if it were necessary.

Under torture, the young woman stated "having Judaized and having gone over with all her heart under the guard of the Law of Moysen in said city of New Veracruz, being more or less eight years old and of having taught her with some rites and ceremonies a certain observant woman that she had named…"

She little confessed about other people, she insisted that she did not know whether her relatives followed the Law of Moses because she had not seen them do so; that she did it by herself and had never talked about it to anybody. She denied what witnesses had said and firmly denied having communicated through the walls of the jail.

In jail she continued with her fasts and traditions, because one prisoner reminded the others using false words; fasts were called "balloons or vanilla" and the money that had been confiscated or they still kept hidden someplace "the georges".

After a number of audiences, Violante accepted having communicated with her relatives and having bribed the guards, accepted having Judaized and begged forgiveness so she would be hurt no more.

Violante Texoso was declared "Heretic, apostate, Judaizer, abettor and of concealing heretics and having gone over to the cursed perverse and dead

Law of Moysen and its followers, believing to be saved in it and so having fallen and incurred in sentence of major excommunication and in the other punishments and unfitness in which fall and incur the heretics that under the name and title of Christians do and commit such crimes and in confiscation and loss of their assets which we apply to the Chamber and Treasury of His Majesty and his receptor in his name since the day and time in which she committed said crimes whose statement we reserve and anyway with good conscience we were able to condemn in the punishments and rights established against such heretics, more attentive to what said Violante Texoso in the confessions she made before us.

We condemn her to jail and perpetual habit of this city and every Sunday and feasts to be kept she should listen to mass and sermon when they have them in the Cathedral Church she with the other penitents. And Saturdays on pilgrimage to the church to be indicated on her knees and with great devotion she should pray five times the Pater Noster with the Ave Maria Creed and Salve Regina and to confess and receive the Saint Sacrament at the altar.

The three Church holidays, the days she will live and we also condemn her to perpetual exile precisely from these Western islands and from the city of Seville, Villa de Madrid Court of His Majesty. And she should embark to comply in the first fleet that from the Port of San Juan de Ulúa should leave to return to the Spanish Kingdoms and that when she arrives in those kingdoms within a month she should present herself at the tribunal of the Holy Office of the Inquisition of Seville, to be recognized and knowledge is taken of her person and she be indicated the part in which she must comply with what is remaining of her habit and jail and so that, in case of contravention, they may proceed against said Violante Texoso, as contra impenitent and relation is sent of this her sentence and condemnation with the signals to the illustrious and most reverend mister General Inquisitor and lords of the council of his majesty of the Holy General Inquisition and to the tribunals of said Inquisition of Seville and of the cities of Lima, Cartagena in these Western Indies.

And it declares to said Violante Texoso for her not to wear, not on her person, gold, silver, pearls nor precious stones, nor silk, camlet, nor fine cloth, nor go on horseback and we declare her unfit and we make her descendants unfit to the degree that according to common right, laws and pragmatics of these kingdoms, and instructions of the Holy Office of the Inquisition be declared unfit to obtain dignities, benefits nor ecclesiastic office, lay whether public or honored, nor to exercise, nor to use of the other things which are forbidden, all of which we order done and to comply under punishment of relapsed impenitent. And for this our definitive sentence judging it we so pronounce and send in these writings and for them."

Don Francisco de Estrada y Escovedo

Don Bernabé de la Higuera y Amarillo

Don Juan Sáenz de Mañozca

The sentence was read out to her in public Auto-da-fe celebrated at the cemetery of the Convent of Santo Domingo, in Mexico City on April 16, 1646. Don Antonio de Gaviola (attorney of the Holy Office) and Violante Texoso, with the insignia which she had to wear, were present. At the end of said Auto, Violante publicly abjured of the crimes of heresy that she had confessed in her process, saying what she was ordered to say and sign:

"I Violante Texoso, originally from Lima in the kingdom of Peru and living in New Veracruz, am here present before Y. H. as apostolic inquisitors that you are against heresy and iniquity and apostasy in Mexico City, I submit to the correction and severity of the sacred canons, so that in me as a person guilty of such crime of heresy be executed the censures and punishments contained in it and from now till then and from then till now they be given and executed in me and I should suffer them when something should be proven having broken of what was said by me abjured and I beg the present secretary that he give it to me as demon and those present are witnesses...."

Her few goods were confiscated, because she lived with her relatives and maintained herself by sewing. Although the sentence did not send her to the stake, it was like life in death, because habit and jail were forever.

The powerful Diego Muñoz de Alvarado

We have given the adjective of powerful to this fervent Jew from Puebla because his financial activities went beyond the limits of the borders of the kingdom of New Spain.

Although he lived in Puebla de los Angeles, he had contact with the converts of the capital and of almost all the Mexican territory.

After having closed off his case, there still appeared several later volumes of debts collected on his goods, besides the collections being made by the Holy Office for confiscation of goods of Don Diego Muñoz de Alvarado, Judaizer.

Don Diego was born in the city of Popayán, Peru. His parents had originally been Portuguese; they went to the kingdom of Peru where they formed a family. From Popayán, they went to New Spain, residing in the city of Puebla. The family was scattered all over the world, because some had remained in Spain, some in Portugal, others in Amsterdam and the rest in America.

Diego would travel to Spain where one of his relatives was administrator of salt in the city of Soria; he would go to the city of Pastrana, sometimes to Bayonne in France, where he had family and friends who continued living as Jews. In Bayonne, there was a synagogue and Jews could live freely as Jews. But there was something that made him always return to America in spite of the dangers to which he was exposed as Judaizer.

Luck had been with him, he had the means to live well and constantly helped a brother who lived in Seville and who was in a terrible economic situation. He was anxious to gather more wealth to help his poor relatives in Spain and all together go to Bayonne to live freely in the Law of Moses.

He was very efficient in his business dealings and he knew that if he was ever apprehended by the Tribunal all his goods would be confiscated. Thus, for "sending money and material in great quantities he availed himself of other people, in whose head there were those shipments, they gave orders and consignations, as if the wealth were theirs, like the shipments to Castile and their jobs, as for their return and remittance, like to that effect this prisoner had performed in the fleet of General Don Gaspar de Velasco sending in it a considerable amount of cochineal in head of a certain friend of his who gave the consignations and orders to benefit from it as if it were his, and the same had happened with certain arrobas or cochineal that were sent to Havana in the year eighty one, so they would go in galleons to the kingdoms of Spain, that this prisoner should have declared the end, cause and reason that he had of availing himself of another's head."[112]

The Holy Office realized the way Diego Muñoz was acting when they confiscated his goods and they saw written down a considerable amount of money in a document from Alvarado that he had given a relative that went through the hands of a royal actuary in Mexico City, "who at the time of absence he made from the Kingdoms of Castile, in the general power that he had left with a certain person very close to collect all the amounts that were owed him, he made a statement at a later date of said power which he said was his will, that none of the empowered people could collect said certain amount from this prisoner, but only in case of death of the mentioned person."

The prisoner died in jail and so the Tribunal found out about many assets that belonged to him that he had not declared as his when he was arrested.

---

[112] A.G.N.M., R.I., T. 644, exp.3

Diego Muñoz had always lived in the fear of falling in prison for professing his faith and he wanted his wife and children to be insured so they would have enough to live on in his absence. His fear became worse when he heard about his brother having been jailed in the city of Seville two weeks before he himself was apprehended.

He asked a relative to "take and keep in his house a certain considerable amount of silver and money that he gave him in this way of hiding his goods he demonstrated the fear of which this prisoner was of being jailed…"

A few days before being captured he gave his wife "ten deeds and a bond in her favor for a considerable amount; and he had scratched out and erased the reasons for them that he had set down in his account book, writing down on the margin of every deed and bond that it was paid."

Diego Muñoz de Alvarado was a rich man; he made his fortune in New Spain devoting himself to carrying merchandise from Holland to England, besides Spain. He had his own vessels that sailed over the ocean in both directions. This is the way it appears in volume 633 of the Archives: "Autos about collection of the merchandise that came in the fleet of last year of 683 belonging to the goods sequestered from Diego Muñoz de Alvarado, preceded by the grace that took to Spain Captain Don Martín de Vallarta in the name of Don Alonso de Vallarta, his brother neighbor of Puebla."[113]

Don Diego was originally from Madrid, legitimate son of Pedro de Alvarado alive at that time, and Doña Sebastiana Pérez already deceased. About his parents there is some confusion perhaps encouraged by Diego himself. During his process, he constantly changed the information, sometimes saying his place of origin being one, then another one and that he was a direct descendant of conqueror Alvarado, that his ancestors had been settlers and conquerors of the kingdoms of Peru.

---

[113] *Ibidem,* Vol. 663, exp. 7 (127 sheets where his goods are mentioned).

What is evident is that Don Diego was a Judaizer and that his parents had been the same; that he arrived from the city of Popayán in Peru and that he was perhaps originally from Spain.

Three relatives of Alvarado had been reconciled and punished for observing the Law of Moses in the "General Auto celebrated in Madrid around the year 1680 and all were from the Portuguese nation, so they knew this prisoner to be from that nation, that generally in the quality and lowness of this prisoner we presume a stain of Judaism."[114]

After he was apprehended in the city of Puebla and taken to the Inquisition in Mexico City, Diego remained during many sessions in audience without talking and unwilling to confess absolutely anything. He constantly feigned being sick, he wouldn't eat, "he was unable to go up to the audience".

He was taken to the torture chamber where he confessed: "Having been doubtful about our Holy Catholic Faith and whether it was good for him or not for his salvation to be observant of said Law of Moses, in which doubt he had been until he received a letter from September thirty of eighty one, from a certain very close person on that date in Seville where he referred that God Our Lord had made many prodigies and mercies for him and not having paid attention to his guilt He had given full recognition of his erring life, habits and steps and that he was just trying for his salvation and to repair his life, asking this prisoner to take care and repair all his actions and that the best joy he could have would be to receive a letter from this prisoner, that would say his having done the same giving away the world and its lies; so that from these admonitions and doubts in which he had fallen or been.... he inferred the observance he had had of said Law of Moses and how obstinate he had been in it..."

---

[114] *Ibidem,* Vol. 664, exp. 3 (All the quotations beginning on this page refer to same archive).

The letter received by Alvarado was from his brother living in Seville, because he had frequent correspondence with him. In it, each encouraged the other of never forgetting either the Law or Jewish religion.

He always simulated being ignorant about what he was asked, because he knew that talking too much could mean prison for any of his relatives or friends whether in the New World or in the Iberian Peninsula.

When he was examined by physicians in prison, his circumcision became evident. He continued fasting and eating only the diet allowed while in jail. After torture he admitted "having lived and living guarding and observing said Law of Moses and that he wanted to die in it…"

He was accused of "perjury, negativity, simulating fake Christianity and of covering up Judaizer heretics". At the beginning he was sentenced for being "heretic Judaizer, apostate of our Holy Catholic Faith and for having incurred in great sentence of excommunication and being linked to it, condemned to the greatest and gravest punishments installed against such criminals by right, laws and pragmatics of these kingdoms, apostolic papal bulls, instructions and letters agreed upon of this Holy Office, so that his crimes are duly punished and may serve as an example to others."

Alvarado was a practical man of affairs who understood perfectly well the consequences of accusing other people or revealing facts that could compromise others. He knew the way the Holy Tribunal managed matters from hearing and seeing other people's experiences.

From the moment when he was led into the secret jail of the Inquisition, he stated that he was sick, that his health was delicate and so he refused to present himself before the inquisitors.

His name until the age of 25 had been Diego Muñoz because that was the way he had been baptized, later he changed his last name to Alvarado. According to his confession, his mother's name was Sebastiana Pérez de Alvarado, resident of the city of Popayán, in Peru. Before she died, she told him that he was son of a clergyman, just like some of his other brothers, and thus, he was not son of Pedro Muñoz, because he had another wife in the kingdoms of Castile.

It is difficult to know whether in reality Diego was the son of a clergyman; what is true is that this bothered the inquisitors, as he argued that he was not of new Christian origin, but rather son of a clergyman and old Christian, who should have carried out his chastity vows.

Alvarado said that his mother had been born in Popayán and was "quadroon, daughter of Spaniard and Mestiza (half breed)."

He insisted very much on his origin; he said that his maternal grandmother was a main Indian "daughter of a Chief" and that none of his relatives had been jailed, reconciled or condemned by the Inquisition.

Since he was very young, he began to travel to Spain, particularly to the port of Cadiz and then to Seville from where he took merchandise to the new World. He would arrive in Veracruz, where he stayed for some time and from there, he continued on to Popayán and Guatemala where he had business.

Every time he arrived in Veracruz, he would get in contact with the community of converts living there, because all of them had always been ready to help him in whatever was necessary. While there they helped him find a wife; she was living in the city of Puebla and so it was that he decided to live definitely in New Spain.

Don Diego was well known in the city of Puebla de los Angeles. He was much liked because he was always willing to help the needy, whether old or new Christian. He took great care not to do anything that looked like Judaizing, but he never forgot his religion. At home and away from the eyes of servants, he religiously kept all the Jewish rites and ceremonies.

He got to occupy important positions in the city of Puebla, having been ordinary mayor of that place.

There was a niece living in his home, whom he had considered putting into a convent as a nun thus confirming his faith in Catholicism in front of others.

Don Diego was an educated man, intelligent, but he had doubts that corroded his soul and, according to him, he devoted himself to constantly writing to people knowledgeable in the Law of Moses to help him work out his problems and confirm his salvation through said Law.

He knew that in Amsterdam converts could practice their Judaism openly and he was anxious to be able to do the same, if only for a couple of weeks. In Holland he sought his fellow Jews; he felt newly Jewish, practiced his rites and returned with new strength to New Spain, where he continued with his double life.

His obsession about silencing the truth led him to become seriously ill while in jail; he would abstain from eating, he said that he had terrible stomachaches.

As a Spaniard, he always referred to his prestigious lineage, remarking on his family relationship to Alvarado the conqueror. This way he believed he could demonstrate the great services that his family had given the Spanish Crown, so he would not be labeled convert.

He performed his business in New Spain and had contact with other cities of the new World. He would take cloth from France and order white clothing (perhaps to be used to wrap bodies in the Jewish manner) and sold it throughout the country.

Besides all the ills from which he said he suffered, he contracted severe pneumonia while in jail that led him to his death.

Very few prisoners had a lawyer to defend them, but Diego Muñoz de Alvarado was able to get one for his defense. The lawyer advised him to "say and confess the truth without raising other under testimony and if he was blamed to ask for penitence, because it would be granted with mercy", but the accused persisted in his obdurate silence, not saying a word about anything; "this prisoner was persistent in not answering straight out to anything that was proposed to him". The lawyer desisted of his purpose because the prisoner stuck firmly to "his errors".

While very sick in jail they had sent a confessor whom he did not accept, "the confessor trying to induce him to the right way, this prisoner having always been persistent and obstinate in not answering straightaway to what his lawyer proposed, because he had misbehaved so he refused to defend him; and although afterward this prisoner had been admonished charitably by us in his jail, being sick he had not requested either confessor or penitence for his crimes, in which state he had ended up his sad and miserable days, negative, stubborn and impenitent."

A public edict was ordered where Alvarado's memory was defamed, mentioning that his stigma would fall upon all his family. This edict was read publicly in Mexico City and Puebla and was published in all the churches.

As a consequence, it stated: "we must declare and do declare that said Diego de Alvarado, alias Muñoz, during the time that he lived and died, having perpetrated and committed the crimes of heresy and apostasy of which he was accused and having been and died heretic, Judaizer, observer of the Law of Moses, apostate, abettor, covering up heretics excommunicated by major excommunication and thus we declare and pronounce and damage his memory and fame; and we declare all his assets confiscated for the Chamber and Treasury of his Majesty and if necessary we apply and to his receptor in his name, from the day and time that he committed said crimes (whose declaration we reserve) we order that on the day of the Auto, he be taken out to the Auto in statue that represents his person, with a shield and habit of the condemned and on the other a sign of the name of said Diego de Alvarado, alias Muñoz, which after this sentence being read publicly he be delivered to the justice and lay arm and his bones be disinterred from the area where they are and delivered to said justice so they will be publicly burned as hatefulness of such serious crimes and to take away and extirpate any title if there were any over his tomb, or arms if they were placed or painted somewhere, so there will be no memory remaining of said Diego de Alvarado, alias Muñoz, on the face of the earth....we declare that the sons and daughters and grandchildren on the masculine side of said Diego de Alvarado, alias Muñoz, be deprived of all and any dignities, benefits and offices, whether ecclesiastic or secular, whether public or honorific, that they have or owned and as unfit and incapable of having others and for being able to ride a horse, bear arms, silk, camlet and fine cloth, gold, silver, precious stones and corals and to exercise and use of the other things that by common right, laws and pragmatics of these kingdoms and instructions of the Holy Office, are forbidden to the children and descendants of such criminals...."

Signatures

Juan Gómez de Mier

Att. Joseph de Omaña Pardo

The sentence was pronounced on February 8, 1688 at the Church of Santo Domingo in Mexico City. After having read it, the secretary and the Main Constable went out carrying the statue and the box of bones of Diego de Alvarado. They went towards the plaza of Santo Domingo where, next to the customs house, the stand where the City Magistrate, don Juan Núñez de Villavicencio and the public actuary Joseph del Castillo were waiting for justice to be done.

The bones and the effigy were condemned to be publicly burned at the incineration area at the Alameda, in the plaza of San Diego. So the bones and the statue were carried through the streets and then burned till they became ashes.

A few days later, the edict was also placed in the city of Puebla together with the figure of Diego Muñoz de Alvarado with the insignia of the condemned.

The assets confiscated from Alvarado were very many. He had held an important position in Puebla society, to the point where no document of blood purity had ever been required from him when he was named ordinary mayor. His life and his work were lost in the course of time. Although he was a good man and always willing to help the fallen, his end was very sad. Nobody in his family ever dared defend his memory because of fear of the Inquisition.

He died without ever having denounced anyone and the only things he confessed were about his Judaism. There is no doubt that he was a good and devoted Jew.

All these processes have one common characteristic: they did not accept religious intolerance as a fatality; they opposed it. As Spaniards they were totally pervaded with religious fervor and fanaticism, although in their case, their passion was for the Jewish religion and not for the Christian one.

Former site of the Inquisition in Mexico

EPILOGUE

Jews arrived in Spain at a very early time in history. According to information obtained, they settled in the Iberian Peninsula since the 1ˢᵗ century of the Common Era; even today tombstones and documents testify to this fact.

There were Jewish families in Spain that alluded to their direct descent from King David and stated that they had arrived in the country after the fall of the first Temple (586 B.C.).

Jews adapted to Spanish soil from the first days of their arrival in the peninsula and they chose Spain as their country of adoption.

In Spanish history, at least up to the time of the expulsion, they occupied a prominent place in the development and evolution of the peninsula.

Jews appear throughout Spanish historiography as a circumstance, not as an integral part of society, at least until the 15ᵗʰ century, when they were expelled from it.

Together with all the inhabitants of the Iberian Peninsula, they developed its spirit and its personality, which would be characteristic over the years and centuries: a special personality of "being Spaniard". There was no great difference whether one was Jewish, Christian or Moslem; being Spanish came before everything else.

Jews soon became a "foreign body" in Spanish society that was in the process of formation. Under the rule of the Visigoths, civil and ecclesiastic power went hand in hand in the desire to attain political and religious unity of Spain.

As the Christian religion came forth, it sharply divided Jews from Catholics. Many were forced to convert and thus the first "converts" from Judaism appeared.

The history of Jews in Spain during the century preceding the arrival of the Moslems is a tale of oppression interrupted by brief periods of tolerance.

The Moslem conquest was a decisive fact in the history of Spanish Jewry. An era of liberty and opportunity opened up; they cultivated their intellect and created new work sources without setting aside their traditions and habits.

During the centuries that the Islamic empire reigned in the peninsula, Jewish culture was reborn assuming a character of excellence. The development of science and literature among the Hebrews placed Spanish Judaism at the forefront of all Jewish communities of Western Europe.

Jews contributed Oriental elements that cemented a synthesis of Arabic sensibility, their pragmatic culture with the Jewish strain of spirituality thus creating a Golden Era.

The figure of the Jew was always present in Spanish courts. Although they continued being faithful to their religion, they exercised considerable authority over the inhabitants of the kingdom. These men were masters and counselors in every phase of life.

Their presence and importance not only impelled popular suspicions but movements organized by intellectuals and people of the church hierarchy also began appearing against the Jews, in which a very critical situation developed. The study of Cabbalah and Zohar intensified seeking for a response to the number of doubts that emerged. Little by little Jews became mystics with definite messianic ideas.

After the reconquest of Spanish territory from the hands of the Moslems, an exaggerated religiosity appeared among the Christians and Catholic Spaniards who were permeated by national feelings of religion, conceiving them in such a way that they were unable to find a central path in their intolerance to the point of later confusing nationality with religion.

Strong individualism and a weak sense of the collective made envy go overboard in Spain and so all the killings and slaughter against Jews and later against new Christians became a reality.

After such tremendous religious oppression, mass conversions of Jews who sought to save their lives appeared in the form of "marranos, convert Crypto-Jews or new Christians."

Every persecution renewed among them the old idea of the arrival of the Messiah. Cabbalists emerged looking for the divine essence and man's destiny. They were anxious to know the signs that forecast the arrival of the Messiah and the redemption of the suffering people.

At various times, this strange knowledge stimulated messianic movements that through desperate efforts gave renewed hope and expectations. They concentrated in the traditional wisdom of the people and, led by their heart's desire and fantasy, turned towards the mysteries and speculations of the Cabbalah and the Zohar.

Converts appeared in the course of Spanish history as a predominant factor in the development of culture and society, totally apart from Jews, Christians or Moslems.

With the ambivalent desire of being able to integrate and at the same time not willing to forget their religion, converts formed a separate social class, different from what had up to then been accepted. With their specific axial table, with an ontological scale like Christians or Moslems, they felt deeply rooted in a millennial culture, but they accepted features of the recently imposed culture.

The tight situation of Jews in relation to Christians during the 15th century was decisive to determine the path of Spanish life. Aspiring to political and religious unity of the Spanish kingdom, Jews were expelled from Spain. This expulsion coincided exactly with the discovery of America. For the convert,

America meant the search for salvation, the arrival of the Messiah in a land that could well have been the "New Jerusalem". Seeing omens and symbols in their expulsion from their beloved Spain, they considered that Jehovah would soon send their redemption because the long expected and dreaded catastrophe had arrived.

The Indies were perhaps the adequate place for the Messiah's birth. And so, many converts decided to risk their lives and small fortunes and to launch forth to the American odyssey, where they hoped to find a longed for peace.

Converts arriving in America were, on one hand, renaissance men with very advanced socio-economic ideas, with a capitalist mentality, interested in the discoveries and culture; and, on the other, they still kept much of the medieval: the sense of honor, deep religiosity, defense of orthodoxy and faith.

Jewish Spaniards were at the same time Jewish and Spanish. They considered dignity and honor important and before anything else, respect to religion. Life was not the supreme good; they were willing to lose it with enthusiasm and to firmly confront death for the sake of an ideal. Death meant the immortality of the soul and this constituted a deep concern.

Discipline, loyalty, religious obedience to laws and tradition, the generous disdain of one's own life and perseverance were not qualities exclusive of Christian Spaniards but were also definite characteristics of Hispano Jews.

Converts who arrived in America were infused, just like Christians, with a messianic feeling which for one was the search for salvation and for the other the transmission of a message in the newly conquered lands. Repression of Judaism only provoked an exaltation of religious practices and an awakening of messianic fervor inherited from their ancestors.

Jews during the Colony tended to gather under a system similar to a "secret society". They promoted among the young generation the love and total surrender to the Law of Moses.

Crypto-Jews taught their children not to despair of the future and to keep alive the hope of a better and fairer world. Armed with an inner strength that bordered on mysticism, Jewish life showed an incredible capacity of recovery and renewal.

The economic roots of their existence were always suspended in air, but their spiritual roots were deeply imbedded in the soil of a vital faith and creative tradition. From this faith and tradition the scheme of a life complete in itself arose, supplied by practices and institutions that had gone through the test and experience of centuries that nourished the mind and spirit of a people.

The color and vitality that characterized the inner life of converts flowed mostly on Sabbath and holidays.

Converts formed part of the social, political and economic life of New Spain. Creating work openings, developing all types of jobs, they integrated into their new situations occupying important positions within Christian life.

Crypto-Jews never forgot their traditions and culture; their problem was to be able to transmit to future generations so they would not forget their historic past and would continue with their love of Jehovah. To die in the holy name of God became the desire of a great part of converts, particularly during the 17th century.

The Spanish Inquisition represented a political measure of Catholicism and originated the Diaspora without which Spanish Jews of the 16th and 17th centuries would have been unable to introduce their vital impulse of religiosity into Holland, England or America.

Throughout the three centuries in which the Holy Office functioned as a tribunal, there were many cases of processed Judaizers. Each one is a complete history of devotion, perseverance and idealism. Each one tells of a life full of sadness and joy, of a struggle to adapt to a new world, different and usually hostile towards converts, towards those that did not have "blood purity". However, there is always a common denominator, their Idealism and

Perseverance in the Law of Moses, denominator that persists throughout the three centuries of domination in New Spain. Whether the victim was processed in the 16th or the 17th century, they all kept a common Ideal of their love to Jewish traditions and culture; their respect for the Law and their utter determination of losing their life in behalf of that Ideal that was considered sacred. In the processes studied there was no difference whether they were tavern keepers, seamstresses or powerful merchants, they were Jews before anything else. Sex or age did not matter, they were all rooted in Jewish customs and traditions learned from infancy.

Although in many cases the sentence was not of "relaxation" (death by fire), it still meant in every way life in death and yet they persisted in their Judaism. Reality was not always condemned to remain as the simple shadow of an ideal. Converts considered that the vacuum between ideal and reality was not absolute or eternal, but that it could and would be overcome by the Messiah. Their idea of God meant the conviction that this messianic struggle would conclude with the establishment of the kingdom of God on Earth.

"Group ideas and ideals may give them some sense, but it is group habits that give them life, because naked ideas are fragile and often succumb when transplanted to a new area; but the idea that has been bedecked by a mantle has much less risk of dying off.

A people in exile, fortified only by concepts, would have finally lost both concepts and its own existence; but a people linked by a community of Law, ritual and behavior, is conceivable to save its Law, its Ideas and even itself".[115]

---

[115] Steinberg, Milton, *La Formación del Judío Moderno,* México, edited by WIZO, 1963, p. 48, 288 pp.

BIBLIOGRAPHY

Actas del primer simposio de estudios sefardíes, primero de los actos celebrados con motivo del XXV aniversario de la Fundación del Consejo Superior de Investigaciones Científicas, edición a cargo de Jacob M. Hassan, con la colaboración de Ma. Teresa Rubiato y Elena Romero, Madrid, Instituto Arias Montano, 1970, 780 pp, XXVI.

Adler, Cyrus, *The trial of Jorge de Almeida*, Publication of the American Jewish Historical Society, núm. 4, 1894.

Albanés, Ricardo, *Los judíos a través de los siglos, historia, religión, psicología y política de Israel*, México, 1939, 478 pp.

Alessio Robles, Vito, *Coahuila y Texas en la época colonial*, México, Ed. Cultura, 1939.

Almoina, José, *Rumbos heterodoxos en México*, Ciudad Trujillo, Ed. Montalvo, 1947, 234 pp.

Alvarez, Jesús P., *Judíos y cristianos ante la historia*, España, Ed. Aguilar, 1972, Col. literaria Tolle, Lege, 378 pp.

Amador de los Ríos, José, *Historia social, política y religiosa de los judíos de España y Portugal*, 2 vols., Buenos Aires. Ed. Bajel, 1943.

Atkinson, William C., *A history of Spain and Portugal*, England, Penguin Books Ltd., 1970, 382 pp.

Baer, Yitzhak Fritz, *Die Juden im christlichen Spanien*, Farnborough, Gregg, Ed. Erster Teil, 1970.

Bamberger, Bernard J. , *The story of judaism*, New York, Schocken Books, 1971, 484 pp.

Baron Wittmayer, Salo, *A social and religious history of the Jews*, XIV vols., New York, Columbia University Press, The Jewish Publication Society of America, 1969 (vol. XIII *Inquisition Renaissance and Reformation*).

Bataillon, Marcel, *Erasmo y España*, México, Fondo de Cultura Económica, 1966, 922 pp.

"Santo Domingo era Portugal" en *Historia y sociedad en el mundo de habla española*, homenaje a José Miranda; Bernardo García Martínez et al. Editores, México, El Colegio de México, 1970, pp. 113-120.

Beinart, Haim, *Anusim bdin ainkvizitzia* (Conversos ante la Inquisición), Tel Aviv, Israel, The Hebrew University of Jerusalem, 1965, 324 pp.

Judíos en las cortes reales de España, Buenos Aires, Ed. Congreso Judío Latinoamericano, 1975, Col. Hechos de la historia judía, núm. 78, 30 pp.

Los comienzos del judaísmo español, Buenos Aires, Ed. ConUeso Judío Latinoamericano, Biblioteca Popular Judía, núm. 62, 32 pp.

Records of the trials of the Spanish Inquisition in ciudad Real (The trials of 1483-1485), Jerusalem, The Israel National Academy of Sciences and Humanities, 1974, 638 pp

"Judíos y conversos en Casarrubias del Monte", en *Homenaje a Juan Prado*, Madrid, 1975, pp. 645-659.

"The converso community in the 16th and 17th century Spain", *The Sephardi heritage*, Edited by R.D. Barnet, London, 1971, pp. 457-478.

"La formación del mundo sefaradí", Conferencia sustentada en la Universidad Iberoamericana, octubre de 1973.

"Los conversos en el siglo XV", Conferencia sustentada en Wizo, México, octubre de 1973.

"La sociedad hispano-judía", Conferencia sustentada en la UNAM, octubre de 1973.

"Salomón Ibn Gabirol y su contexto histórico" en Revista *Seis conferencias en torno a Ibn Gabirol*, Málaga, Ed. A. Cano, 1973, pp. 5-10.

Bension, Ariel, *El Zohar en la España musulmana y cristiana*, Madrid, Compañía Iberoamericana de Publicaciones, Renacimiento, 193 1, 331 pp.

Bernáldez, Andrés, *Antología, Memorias del reinado de los Reyes Católicos*, Selec. y prol., Octavio de Madeiras, Madrid, Ed. Fe, 1945, 316 pp.

Borges, Ana Lola, "La mujer pobladora en los orígenes americanos", Sevilla, Separata del T. XXIX del *Anuario de Estudios Americanos*, 1972, pp. 389-444.

Bravo Ugarte, José, *Historia de México, La Nueva España*, 2 vols., 4a. ed., México, Ed. Jus, 1960, 354 pp.

Brenner, Anita, "Cavaliers and martyrs" in *Menorah Journal*, 16 de enero de 1929.

Brom, Juan, *Para comprender la historia*, México, Ed. Nuestro Tiempo, S.A., 1972, 172 pp.

Cantera Burgos, Francisco, "Los sefardíes, fermento de espiritualidad en el judaísmo", en *España*, núm. 32, 1949, pp. 12 Y 13.

Capdequi Ots, J.M. *El Estado español en las Indias*, 4a. ed., México, Fondo de Cultura Económica, 1965, 184 pp.

Carreño, Alberto María, "Luis de Carvajal el Mozo", en *Memorias de la Academia de la Historia de México*, núm. 15, enero-marzo de 1956, pp. 87-101.

Carter, C., *Law and society in colonial México; Audiencia judges in Mexican society. The Tello de Sandoval Visita General* (1543-1547), Columbia University (Ph. D.), 1971, 190 pp (University Microfilm, Ann Arbor, Michigan).

Carvajal, Luis de, *Procesos de Luis de Carvajal el Mozo*, México, Talleres Gráficos de la Nación, 1935, 537 pp.

Casas, Bartolomé de las (Ob. de Chiapas), *Historia de las Indias*, 2 vols., México, Ed. José M. Vigil, 1877.

Castro, Américo, *La realidad histórica de España*, México, Ed. Porrúa, S.A., 1954, 684 pp.

Los españoles, cómo llegaron a serlo, Madrid, Taurus Ediciones, 1965, Col. Ser y   Tiempo, núm. 1, 298 pp.

España en su historia, cristianos, moros y judíos, Buenos Aires, s.e., 1948.

Cue Cánovas, Agustín, *Historia social y económica de México, 1521-1854*, México, Trillas, 1973, 422 pp.

Cuevas, Mariano (Padre), *Historia de la Iglesia en México*, 5 vols., 5a. ed., México, Ed. Patria, 1946., ils.

Davies, Trevor, *La decadencia española*, 1621-1700, Barcelona, Labor, 1969, 190 pp.

Díaz del Castillo, Bernal, *Historia verdadera de la conquista de la Nueva España, Introducción y notas de Joaquín Ramírez Cabañas*, Ed. Porrúa, S.A., 1960, 648 pp.

Diccionario Porrúa, *Historia, biografía y geografía de México*, 3a. ed., México, Ed. Porrúa, S.A., 1970.

Dimont, Max 1., *Los judíos, Dios y la historia*, trad. de Goldie B. de Chelminsky, México, Ed. Menorah.,s.f., 502 pp.

Domínguez Ortiz, Antonio, *El antiguo régimen, los Reyes Católicos y los Austrias*, Madrid, Alianza Editorial, Alfaguara, 1973, 490 pp.

Dorantes de Carranza, Baltazar, *Sumaria relación de las cosas de la Nueva España*, México, Ed. José María de Ageda y Sánchez, 1902.

Dubnow, Simón, *Historia universal del pueblo judío*, trad. de León Dujovne, IO vols., Buenos Aires, Ed. S. Sigal, 1951.

Dujovne, León. *La filosofía de la historia en la antigüedad y en la Edad Media*, Buenos Aires, Ediciones Galatea, Nueva Visión, 1958, Col. El hombre, la sociedad y la historia, 246 PP.

Enciclopedia Judaica Castellana, "El pueblo judío en el pasado y en el presente", IO vols., México, Ed. Enciclopedia Judaica Castellana, S. de R.L., 1950.

Encyclopedia Judaica Jerusalem, 16 vols., New York, The Macmillan Company, 1971 (produced and printed in Jerusalem, Israel), ils. maps., fots.

Estrugo, José M., *Los sefardíes*, La Habana, Ed. Lex, 1958, 144 pp.

Fernández del Castillo, Francisco, *Libros y libreros en el siglo XVI (documentos)*, México, Guerrero Hermanos, 1914 (Publicaciones del Archivo General de la Nación, VI)., 608 pp.

Finkelstein, Louis, *The Jews, their history, culture and religion*, 2 vols., New York, Harper Publications, 1949.

Flores Caballero, Romeo, *La contrarrevolución en la Independencia*, México, El Colegio de México, 1969, Centro de Estudios Históricos, Nueva Serie, núm. 8.

Gallegos Rocafull, J.M., *El pensamiento mexicano en los siglos XVI y XVII*, México, UNAM, 1951

García, Genaro, Carlos Pereyra, "La inquisición de México, sus orígenes, competencia, autos de fe, relaciones con los poderes públicos, ceremonias, etiquetas y otros hechos", en *Documentos inéditos para la historia de México*, T. V, México, 1906, 284 pp.

Gittelsohn, Roland B., *The meaning of Judaism*, New York, The World Publishing Company, Excalibur Books, 1970, 22 pp.

González Obregón, Luis, *México viejo, época colonial*, México, Ed. Patria, 1959, 742 pp.

Graetz, Heinrich, *History of the Jews,* 6 vols., Philadelphia, Jewish Publications Society, 1894.

Grayzel, Salomon, *A history of the Jews*, New York, New American Library, 1968, 768 pp.

Greenleaf, Richard E., "Francisco Millan before the Mexican Inquisition", *in Publication of the Americas*, October 21, 1964.

The Mexican Inquisition of the sixteenth century, Albuquerque, University of New Mexico Press, 1969, 242 pp

Zumárraga and the Mexican Inquisition 1536-1543, Washington, Academy of American Franciscan History, 196 1, 155 pp,

Haring, Clarence H., *Comercio y navegación entre España y las Indias en la época de los Habsburgos*, México, Fondo de Cultura Económica, 1939

Hernández Díaz, José, *El Testamento de Don Hernando Colón y otros documentos para su biografía*, Sevilla, de la Gavidia, 1941, T. XXXIII, 319 pp.

Hernández Ortiz, Rafael, *La Inquisición en México*, México, Imprenta Acción, 1944 (Tesis UNAM, Facultad de Derecho).

Hoskins, L., *Glass and clash in seventeenth century in Mexico*, Michigan, University Microfilms, Ann Arbor, 1974, 238 pp. maps., ils.

Husik, Isaac, *A history of mediaeval Jewish philosophy*, New York, Atheneum, 1969, 466 pp.

Iglesia, Ramón, *El hombre Colón y otros ensayos*, México, El Colegio de México, 1944, Publicaciones del Centro de Estudios Históricos, 306 pp.

Jiménez Rueda, Julio, *Historia de la cultura en México, El Virreinato*, México, Ed. Cultura, 1960, 334 pp.

Herejías y supersticiones en la Nueva España (*Los heterodoxos en México*), Imprenta universitaria, 1946, 306 pp.

Junco, Alfonso, *Inquisición sobre la Inquisición*, México, Ed. Jus, 1949, 309 pp.

Kahler, Erich, *¿Qué es la historia?* trad. de Juan Almela, México, Fondo de Cultura Económica, 1966, Col. Breviarios núm. 187.

Kayserling, Meyer, *Christopher Columbus and the participation of the Jews in the Spanish and Portuguese discoveries*, trad. de Charles Gross, New York, Hermon Press, 1968, 189 pp.

Keller, Werner, *Diaspora, the post-biblical history of the Jews*, New York, Harcourt Brace and World Inc., 1966, 522 pp.

Ketzer, N. Morris, *Principios esenciales de la fe judía*, México, Edición del Instituto de Relaciones Humanas, 1968, Biblioteca Nuestro Tiempo núm. 3, 56 pp.

Lacalle, José María, *Los judíos españoles*, Barcelona, Sayma Ediciones y Publicaciones Panorama A Z, I (La universidad en su mano), 1964, 238 pp.

Landstrom Bjorn, Columbus, *The story of Don Cristobal Colon admiral of the ocean*, New York, The Macmillan Company, 1967, 208 pp.

Lea, Henry Charles, *A history of the Inquisition of Spain*, 4 vols., New York, The Macmillan Company, 1906.

The Inquisition in the Spanish dependencies, New York, The Macmillan Company, 1908, 256 pp.

Learsi, Rufus, *Historia del pueblo judío*, Buenos Aires, Ed. Israel, 1959, Ediciones judías en castellano, vol. LIII, 744 pp.

Lewin, Boleslao, *La Inquisición en Hispanoamérica (judíos, protestantes y patriotas)*, Buenos Aires, Ed. Proyección, 1962, 349 pp.

Los judíos bajo la Inquisición en Hispanoamérica, Buenos Aires, Ed. Dédalo, 1960, 144 pp.

Mártires y conquistadores judíos en la América Hispana, Buenos Aires, Ed. Candelabro, 1954, 276 pp.

La Inquisición en México siglos XVI y XVII, 2 vols., Buenos Aires, Ed. Cajica, 1967.

Liamagot, Alberto, *Cripto-judíos en Hispanoamérica*, Buenos Aires, Editado por el Ejecutivo Sudamericano del Congreso Judío Mundial, 1970, Biblioteca Popular Judía, núm. 31, 32 pp.

Liebman, Seymour B., *A guide to Jewish references in the Mexican colonial era 1521-1821*, Philadelphia, University of Pennsylvania Press, 1964, 134 pp.

The enlightened, the writings of Luis de Carvajal el Mozo, Coral Gables, University of Miami Press, 1967, 160 pp.

Los judíos en México y América Central (fe, llamas e Inquisición), trad. de Elsa C. Frost, Buenos Aires, Siglo Veintiuno editores, S.A., 1971, 482 pp.

Valerosas cripto-judías en la América colonial, Buenos Aires, Biblioteca Popular Judía, núm. 66, 1973, 40 pp.

The inquisitors and the Jews in the New World (Summaries of proceses 1500-1810 and bibliographical guide), Coral Gables Florida, University of Miami Press, 1974, 224 pp., ils.

"Sephardic ethnicity in the spanish new colonies", presentado al Congreso de Americanistas, México, septiembre de 1974, 42 pp.

López Martínez, Nicolás, *Los judaizantes castellanos y la Inquisición en tiempo de Isabel La Católica*, Burgos, Publicaciones del Seminario Metropolitano, 1954, 451 pp.

Luna, Benjamín Laureano, "Los judíos, la Inquisición y la Independencia de México", en Revista *Época*, Publicaciones Quirós, núm. 149, México, 1975, p. 21-38.

Llaverías, Federico, Cristóbal Colón, *El hallazgo de sus restos en Santo Domingo*, La Habana, P. Fernández y Cía., 1939 27 pp

Llorente, Juan Antonio, *La Inquisición y los españoles, Prólogo y notas de Valentina Fernández Vargas*, Madrid, Ed Ciencia Nueva, S.L., 1967, 276 pp.

Madariaga, Salvador, *El ocaso del imperio español en América*, Buenos Aires, Ed. Sudamericana, 1955, 552 pp.

Marcu, Valeriu, *The expulsion of the Jews from Spain*, trad. de Moray Firth, New York, The Viking press, 1935, 181 pp.

Mariel de Ibáñez, Yolanda, *La Inquisición en México durante el siglo XVI*, México, UNAM, 1945, 67 pp (Tesis).

Márquez de Lozoya, *Historia de España*, 5 vols., Barcelona, Salvat Editores, S A. , 1967.

Martínez del Río, Pablo, *El Alumbrado*, México, Porrúa Hermanos, 1937, 197 pp.

Medina, José Toribio, *Historia del Tribunal del Santo Oficio de la Inquisición en México*, 2a. ed., ampliada por Julio Jiménez Rueda, México, Ediciones Fuente Cultural, 1952, 450 pp

Menéndez Pidal, Ramón, *Los españoles en la historia*, Buenos Aires, Espasa Calpe, 1959, 238 pp.

Menéndez y Pelayo, Marcelino, *La mística española*, Estudio preliminar de Pedro Sáenz Rodríguez, Madrid, Ed. A. Aguado, 1956.

Historia de los heterodoxos españoles, Madrid, Biblioteca de Autores Cristianos, 1965, 286 pp.

Millás Vallicrosa, José Ma., "Historia de los judíos españoles" en *Sefarad* V, 1945 pp. 417-440, y núm. 1946 pp. 163-188

Miranda, José, *Vida colonial y albores de la independencia*, México, SEP, 1972, Sepsetentas núm. 56, 252 pp

España y Nueva España en la época de Felipe II, México, UNAM, 1962, 131 pp

Núñez Martínez, Edith, *La influencia judía en la España medieval*, México, UNAM, 1950, 70 pp. (Tesis).

Nwasike Dominic, Azikiwe, *Mexico City town government 1590-1650: study in aldermanic background and performance*, Wisconsin, University Microfilms Inc. Ann Arbor, Michigan, 1972, 282 pp, (Tesis).

O 'Brien, John, The Inquisition, New York, University of Notre Dame, Macmillan Publishing Co. Inc., 1973, 234 pp.

Peers, Edgar Allison, *El misticismo español*, Buenos Aires, Espasa Calpe, 1947, 215 pp.

Pendle, George, *A history of Latin America*, Great Britain, Penguin Books, 1971, 258 pp.

Pereyra, Carlos, *Obras completas*, 2 vols., México, Libreros Mexicanos Unidos, Col. Laurel, 1960.

Pérez, León, *La identidad reprimida, judíos y negros*, Buenos Aires, Galerna, 1968, 286 pp.

Pérez, Lorenzo, *Anales judaicos de Mallorca*, España, Luis Ripoll ed., 1974, 264 pp.

Pérez Marchand, Monelisa Lina, *Dos etapas ideológicas del siglo XVIII en México a través de los papeles de la Inquisición*, México, El Colegio de México, 1945, 237 pp.

Phipps, Helen, "Notes on Medina Ricos Visita de Hacienda to the Inquisition of México", *Separata*, New York, pp. 79-89.

Pinta Llorente, Miguel de la, *La Inquisición española y los problemas de la cultura y de la intolerancia*, 2 vols., Madrid, Ediciones Cultura Hispánica, 1953.

Poliakov, León, *Historia del antisemitismo, desde Cristo hasta los judíos de la corte*, trad. de Susana de Aldecoa, Buenos Aires, Ed. Siglo Veinte, 1968, 334 pp.

Histoire de L'ántisemitisme, de Mahomet aux marranes, Paris, Calmann-Levy, 1961, Collection Liberté de l'esprit, 380 pp.

Prescott, W.H., *Historia del reinado de los Reyes Católicos, Don Fernando y Doña Isabel*, 2 vols., trad de Pedro Sabau Larroyo, México, Tipografía de F. Escalante y Cía., 1854.

Proodian García de, Lucía, *Los judíos en América, sus actividades en los virreinatos de Nueva Castilla y Nueva Granada, siglo XVII*, prólogo de Manuel Ballesteros Gaibrois, Madrid, 1966, 562 pp.

Puigross, Rodolfo, *La España que conquistó el Nuevo Mundo*, Buenos Aires, Ediciones Siglo Veinte, 1965, 222 pp.

Ramos Oliveira, Antonio, *Historia de España*, 2 vols., México, Compañía General de Ediciones, S.A., 1967.

Riva Palacio, Vicente, *México a través de los siglos*, 5 vols., México, Publicaciones Herrerías, s.f.

El Libro Rojo, México, Publicaciones Herrerías, 1867.

Roth, Cecil, *Historia de los marranos*, trad. de Aarón Spivak, Buenos Aires, Ed. Israel, 1941, 323 pp.

San Agustín, *La Ciudad de Dios*, trad. de D. José Cayetano Díaz de Beyral, 4 vols., Madrid, Biblioteca Clásica, 1893.

Scholem, Gershom, *The messianic idea in judaism*, New York, Schocken Books, 1972, 376 pp.

On the Kabbalah and its symbolism, New York, Schocken Books, 1973, 216 pp.

Schwartzman, Pablo, *Judíos en América*, Buenos Aires, Instituto Amigos del Libro Argentino, Col. Ensayos, núm. II, 1963, 140 pp.

Sims, Harold, *The expulsion of the Spaniards from Mexico*, 182 7-1828, Ann Arbor, Michigan, University Microfilms Inc., 1968, 468 pp (Tesis).

Steinberg, Milton, *La formación del judío moderno*, trad. de Goldie B. de Chelminsky, México, Ed. Wizo, 1963, 288 pp.

Suárez Fernández, Luis, *Documentos acerca de la expulsión de los judíos*, Consejo Superior de Investigaciones Científicas, 1964, 564 pp.

Testas, Guy y Jean, *La Inquisición*, trad. de Guillem Frontera, Barcelona, Oikos Tau, 1969, Ediciones Que Sais-Je en lengua castellana, núm. 8, 128 pp.

Torre y del Cerro, José de la, *Beatriz Enriquez de Harana y Cristóbal Colón*, prólogo de Ots Capdequi, Madrid, Compañía Iberoamericana de Publicaciones, 1933, 181 pp.

Torroba Bernaldo de Quiros, Felipe, *Los judíos españoles*, Madrid, s.e., 1967, 366 pp.

Toro, Alfonso, *Los judíos en la Nueva España*, selección de documentos del siglo XVI correspondientes al ramo de Inquisición, México, Talleres gráficos de la nación, 1932, 372 pp.

La familia Carvajal, estudio histórico sobre los judíos y la Inquisición de la Nueva España en el siglo XVI, 2 vols., basado en documentos originales y en su mayor parte inéditos, que se conservan en el A.G.N.M., México, Ed. Patria, 1944.

Trabulse, Elías, *Ciencia y religión en el siglo XVII*, México, El Colegio de México, 1974, Centro de Estudios Históricos, Nueva Serie 18, 286 pp.

Turberville, *La Inquisición española*, México, Fondo de Cultura Económica, 1950, Breviario núm. 2, 154 pp.

Vera, Francisco, *Los judíos españoles y su contribución a las ciencias exactas*, Buenos Aires, El Ateneo, 1948, 250 pp.

Vicens, Vives, *Historia económica y social de América y España*, 5 vols., México, Ed. TYD, 1967.

Zamacois, Niceto de, *Historia de México desde sus tiempos más remotos hasta nuestros días*, 10 vols., México. Ed. Juan de la Fuente Parres, s.f.

Zavala, Silvio, *El mundo americano en la época colonial*, 2 vols., México, Ed. Porrúa, 1967, Biblioteca Porrúa núms. 39 y 40.

| Lote Riva Palacio | | | Tomo | Exp. | Tomo | Exp. | Tomo | Exp. |
Tomo	Exp.	Num. Gral.						
3	1		11	1 y 2	125	2	223	
11		1487	14	33	126	12	227	3
14		1489	18	6	148	2	233	38
20	5	1495	30	1 y 8	150	2	252-A	4
29	6		47	7	151	3	254	
35	2		57	1	152	5	254-A	9
44	2		58	16	153	4	273	2
55	4		59	7	154	2 y 3	274	2
			79	10	157	4	275	4
			80	8 y 20	160	2	289	3, 9, 10,
					161	8 y 13	291	13
					164	2	293	5
					166	3		28
					174	3		
						4		

Tomo	Exp.	Tomo	Exp.	Tomo	Exp.	Tomo	Exp.	Tomo	Exp.
301	48	401	3	540	30	614	8	1408	13
318	9-A	402	2	586	3	621	14	1429	59
335	86	405	9			644	3	1487	11 R.P.
354	27	409	4			652	1, 2, 3	1489	14 R.P.
363	30	411	1			653	1, 2, 3	1495	20 R.P.
365	11 y 33	414	6			654	1 al 10		
373	9	415	5			655			
378	2	416	24			658	3, 4, 5		
381	5 y 9	418	7			663	7		
392	3	426	7			682	5 y 6		
394	2	436	14			684			
395	2, 3, 5	440				689	42		
396	2	453	1						
398	1								

BOLETINES CONSULTADOS			
Boletín A.G.N.M.*	TOMO	AÑO	REFERENTE A:
Boletín	IV	1930	Correspondencia de Luis Carvajal el Mozo con su familia.
Boletín pp. 99-149	VI, núm. 1	1935	Causa criminal contra Tomás Treviño de Sobremonte, judaizante, 1625.
Boletín pp 305-309	VI, núm. 2	1935	Causa criminal contra Tomás Treviño de Sobremonte, 1625.
Boletín 420-465	VI, núm. 3	1935	Causa criminal contra Tomás Treviño de Sobremonte, 1625.
Boletín pp. 578-621	VI, núm. 4	1935	Causa criminal contra Tomás Treviño de Sobremonte, 1625.
Boletín pp. 757-778	VI, núm. 5	1935	Causa criminal contra Tomás Treviño de Sobremonte, por judaizante.
Boletín 88-143	VII, núm. 1	1935	Causa criminal contra Tomás Treviño de Sobremonte, por judaizante.
Boletín pp. 256-273	VII, núm. 2	1936	Causa criminal Tomás Treviño de Sobremonte, por judaizante.
Boletín pp. 402-437	VII, núm. 3	1936	Causa criminal Tomás Treviño de Sobremonte, por judaizante.
Boletín pp. 596-600	VII, núm. 4	1936	Causa criminal Tomás Treviño de Sobremonte.
Boletín (completo) pp. 1-173	VIII, núm. 1	1937	Causa criminal Tomás Treviño de Sobremonte. Concluye.
Boletín pp. 224-233	VIII, núm. 2	1937	Acusación contra Juana Tinoco, por hereje judaizante, apóstata, 1640-1646
Boletín pp. 53-90 pp. 293-316	XXVI	1955	Memoria del Tribunal de la Inquisición de Nueva España, 1571-1656

| Boletín | XXVIII | 1956 | Estrada Pedro de, Autos de fe de la Inquisición de México con extractos de sus causas, 1646-1648 (en García Genaro, Documentos inéditos o muy raros para la historia de México. |

* Boletín del Archivo General de la Nación, México, Talleres gráficos de la Nación, Secretaría de Gobernación. Director Rafael López, jefe de historiadores Luis González Obregón.

ABBREVIATIONS

A.G.N.M	Archivo General de la Nación Mexicana.
R.I.	Ramo Inquisición.
A.I.	Archivo de Indias
E.J.C.	Enciclopedia Judaica Castellana
E.J.J.	Encyclopedia Judaica Jerusalem
Exp.	Expediente
U.H.J.	Universidad Hebrea de Jerusalén
U.N.A.M.	Universidad Nacional Autónoma de México